The History of the Tenth Cavalry, 1866-1921

Compiled and Edited
BY
MAJOR E. L. N. GLASS, 10TH CAV.
COPYRIGHT, 1921

The History of the Tenth Cavalry

1866   1921

COLONEL EDWIN B. WINANS

Dedication

to one who inspires the respect of those
who know him, whose qualities of character
create both affection and personal loyalty,
to one under whom it is a pleasure
and a privilege to serve.

to

Edwin Baruch Winans,
Colonel Tenth Cavalry,

this book is dedicated as a slight tribute
of the regard in which he is held
by his command.

JOHN J. PERSHING
GENERAL OF THE ARMIES

Foreword

The record of the phenomenal growth and expansion of our country is resplendent with the contributory and glorious achievements of its Army. From the pioneer days when our forefathers carved their way into the wilds and dangers of the west to the present, the Army has played a most important part in shaping the destiny of this country. It has been an honor, which I am proud to claim, to have been at one time a member of that intrepid organization of the Army which has always added glory to the military history of America—The 10th Cavalry.

Several years of my early military life were spent with that organization, and as I look back I can but feel that the associations with the splendid officers and men of the 10th Cavalry were of the greatest value to me. The Army and the country must assuredly have a glorious sense of pride when they review through these pages the stirring deeds and honorable history of this Regiment.

It is a pleasure to have this opportunity of recording my congratulations to the officers and men who have been or are members of the 10th Cavalry, not only on their contribution to the Army during the past but also on their present high state of efficiency and organization. My best wishes go with you in the full confidence that you will meet every call which falls to you in the days to come with the same spirit of patriotism and sense of duty as you have in the past.

John J. Pershing

J. G. HARBORD
MAJOR GENERAL, U. S. A.

Introduction

Thirty years ago the Old Army, whose traditions we inherit, was the Indian-fighting army which had won the west for our civilization. After the Spanish-American war it was the service of the period just preceding that conflict. Now a new generation is talking of the Old Army, meaning the regular service as we knew and loved it in the first sixteen years of the century.

But for anyone now in the American uniform, the Tenth Cavalry has always been of the Old Army. It probably has more veterans in its ranks than any other regiment in the service. The traditions of other days cluster round its guidons, and the brave stories of the frontier are still told before its camp-fires.

Organized in 1866, with officers and men fresh from the fields of the Civil War, it bore an honorable part in the hard riding and fighting of the Indian wars. Thirty-four years ago it was scouting the cactus-covered hills of Arizona near where its guidons flutter today, hunting the Apache Kid and Geronimo of the wily Apaches.

A period of garrison life in Montana, enlivened by occasional contact with the ghost-dancing warriors of the North, and the regiment was brought to Tampa in June, 1898, from three different stations. How well it bore its part in the fighting before Santiago is told in every history of the Cuban campaign. From Montauk to Huntsville, thence to Texas, and back to Cuba in April, 1899, kept the regiment busy in the months that followed the surrender of Santiago.

A squadron of the Tenth fought in Samar in the last days of the Philippine insurrection, the remainder of the regiment returning to Texas from Cuba. It followed Pershing into Mexico after the Columbus raid—and there were men in it who remembered when the general had been a lieutenant in the regiment. The years 1917-19 found the Tenth Cavalry along our Mexican frontier exemplifying the fact that no matter what the remainder of the army may be doing, our southern border is as much the responsibility of our cavalry as the defense of our harbors is the duty of the coast artillery, or the ocean is the battlefield and maneuver ground of our army.

In these days of unrest and uncertainty, inevitable after such a war as nearly wrecked our civilization, the rallying points in our service must be in the study of our military history and the preservation of our ancient traditions. There are few regiments in any service which can point to a half century of better history than can the Tenth United States Cavalry, of which the writer is proud that he was once an officer.

Camp Travis, Texas, May 20th, 1921.

J. G. Harbord

Major General, U. S. Army.

Preface

This volume contains the history of the Tenth Cavalry from its organization to present date, so far as can be gleaned from reports, records and personal recollections No effort has been made to elaborate on incidents, the aim being merely to present an accurate and brief record of the regiment

The editor desires to express his thanks and appreciation for the contributions and memoranda received from General John J Pershing, Major General James G Harbord, Brigadier General S L Woodward, Lieutenant Colonel Frederick J Herman, Lieutenant Colonel C A Romeyn, and Lieutenant Colonel E Phillips, and for the valuable assistance rendered by Staff Sergeants James F. Booker and Andrew Lewis

The Birth of the Tenth Cavalry

The sterling worth of the colored soldier was proved on many battlefields of the Civil War. Congress was eminently right in providing for four regiments of colored soldiers, in the reorganization bill of 1866.

Section III of an "Act to Increase and Fix the Military Peace Establishment of the United States", provided "that to the six regiments of cavalry now in service, there shall be added four regiments, two of which shall be composed of colored men". These two became the Ninth and Tenth Regiments of Cavalry.

The Tenth Cavalry on the 28th day of July, 1866, thus came into being, to join her sister regiments among the elite of the army, and in the years that followed, created for itself a record which cedes primacy to none.

Chapter I.

ORGANIZATION AND COMPOSITION

UNTIL Colonel Benjamin H. Grierson arrived at Fort Leavenworth, Kanhas, to organize the regiment, the Tenth Cavalry existed only in the statute books. The Adjutant General of the Army was apprised of its existence upon the receipt of its initial regimental return, dated September 30, 1866.

This return shows the total strength of the regiment to consist of Colonel Grierson, present for duty, and Lieut. Colonel Charles C. Walcutt, absent on recruiting service. The only other entry is "Recruits required, 1092." Recruiting for the regiment, however, was actually carried on throughout the Departments of the Missouri, Arkansas and Platte. Officers were detailed to canvass the colored troops of those departments, and secured re-enlistments for the new regiments. In those days the enlistment period was five years for cavalry service, three years for infantry; an early criterion for the argument that a longer time is required to develop the cavalry soldier.

As regards the officers, Congress had passed a proviso regulating the commissions granted in these new regiments:

"That no person shall be commissioned in any of the regiments authorized by this Act until he shall have passed a satisfactory examination before a board to be composed of officers of that arm of the service in which the applicant is to serve, to be convened under the direction of the Secretary of War, which shall inquire into the services rendered during the war, capacity and qualifications of the applicant; and every such appointment, when made, shall be without regard to previous rank, but with sole regard to qualifications and meritorious services."

There can be no doubt that the above enactment permitted men of only the highest caliber to be commissioned in these regiments. This insured for the infant Tenth Cavalry a splendid body of officers, who gave it a good start in life. The regimental commander, as a corollary, also set a high enlistment standard. So high, in fact, that by the close of the year (1866) but sixty-four recruits had been accepted.

A unique feature of the recruiting was the fact that it was mainly regimental. Officers of the regiment would not wait at headquarters for the recruits to come in; on the contrary, they were sent out to do their own recruiting. In this way applicants for enlistment would see at the start the kind of officer they were to soldier under. Likewise, the officer could see what kind of men he was taking into his regiment, or troop.

The return for December, 1866, shows two field officers, one company officer and sixty-four unassigned recruits. There was as yet no staff, nor any clerks. To remedy the lack of material for the non-commissioned grades, etc., Colonel Grierson had Captain Louis H Carpenter sent to Philadelphia, Pa., writing him

'I requested you to be sent there to recruit colored men sufficiently educated to fill the positions of non-commissioned officers, clerks and mechanics in the regiment. You will use the greatest care in your selection of recruits. Although sent to recruit men for the positions specified above, you will also enlist all superior men you can who will do credit to the regiment.'

In July the regiment comprised

Field and Staff—
    Colonel B H Grierson,
    Lt Col J W Davidson,
    Major J W Forsyth,
    Major M H Kidd,
    Chaplain W M Grimes,
    Captain Henry E Alvord, Adjutant

Company A—Color, bay. Organized February 18, 1867
    Captain Nicholas Nolan,
    Lieut G W Graham,
    Lieut G F Raulston

Company B—Color, bay. Organized April 1, 1867
    Captain J B Vande Wiele,
    Lieut J D Myrick,
    Lieut J W Myers

Company C—Color, bay. Organized May 15, 1867
    Captain Edward Byrne,
    Lieut. T. C. Lebo,
    Lieut T J Spencer

Company D—Color, bay. Organized June 1, 1867, at Fort Gibson, I T
    Captain J. W. Walsh,
    Lieut Robert Gray,
    Lieut R H Pratt

Company E—Color, bay. Organized June 15, 1867
    Captain G T Robinson,
    Lieut J T Morrison

Company F—Color, gray. Organized June 21, 1867
    Captain G A Armes,
    Lieut P L Lee,
    Lieut J A Bodamer

Company G—Color, bay. Organized July 5 1867
    Captain H T Davis,
    Lieut W B Kennedy,
    Lieut M J Amick

Company H—Color, black. Organized July 21, 1867
    Captain L H Carpenter,
    Lieut T. J. Spencer,
    Lieut L H Orleman.

Aggregate strength, 25 officers and 702 men.

On August 6, 1867, regimental headquarters moved to Fort Riley, Kansas, where the remaining four troops were organized, as follows:

Company I—Color, bay. Organized August 15, 1867.
Captain G. W. Graham,
Lieut. Silas Pepoon.

Company K—Color, bay. Organized September 1, 1867.
Captain C. G. Cox,
Lieut. R. G. Smithers,
Lieut. B. F. Bell.

Company L—Color, sorrel. Organized September 2,1 1867.
Captain R. Gray,
Lieut. C. E. Nordstrom.

Company M—Color, mixed. Organized October 15, 1867.
Captain H. E. Alvord,
Lieut. P. L. Lee,
Lieut. W. R. Harmon.

(Company M got all the horses that would not match any other troop and was called the "Calico" company).

The last original vacancies in the field and staff were filled by the assignment of Major J. E. Yard, and the appointment of 1st Lieut. W. H. Beck as regimental quartermaster. The chaplain's duties included instructing the enlisted men in common school subjects. He was a "regimental chaplain';; outside the colored regiments they were "army chaplains."

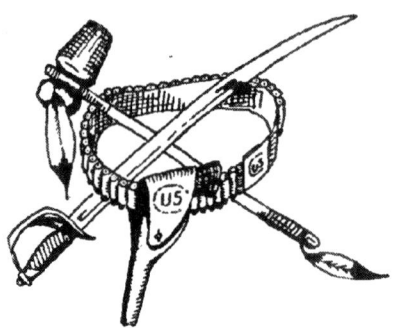

Chapter II.

EARLY FIELD SERVICE

LITTLE time was lost in placing the regiment in the field. The 1st and 2nd Squadrons were detailed on the list of the Kansas Pacific Railroad, guarding it and protecting the working parties. Fort Hays, Fort Harker, and other posts along the Smoky Hill River, Kansas, were the outposts of civilization. Beyond lay the hunting grounds of the Indians, and they looked with dread and anger at the advancement of civilization westward.

The colors of the regiment first came under fire on August 2, 1867, about forty miles northeast of Fort Hays, near the Saline River. Company F, patrolling the railroad, was attacked by a band of three hundred Indians. The troop comprised two officers and thirty-four men. The fight lasted six hours. The troop, badly outnumbered, was in the end forced to retire, after inflicting heavy losses on the hostiles. Captain Armes was wounded, and Sergeant William Christy killed.

On the 21st of the same months the second baptism of fire was had. Captain Armes with forty of his men, together with ninety men of the 18th Kansas Volunteers, engaged some thousand hostiles in about the same locality as the first fight. They were hampered by a large wagon train loaded with supplies. The engagement lasted all the afternoon, with severe losses on both sides. One private of F Company was killed and nineteen wounded. The volunteers lost fifteen wounded. Fifteen horses were killed and many wounded. A first hand account of this engagement would be most valuable; unfortunately, it is doubtful if there survives today any participant.

On September 15th, 1868, a detachment of Company G, Sergeant Davis and nine men, was attacked by sixty Cheyennes. The Indians were badly beaten, with the loss of one private wounded and two laborers killed.

The headquarters of the regiment remained at Fort Riley until April 17, 1868. The regiment was scattered throughout Kansas and Indian Territory (Oklahoma); the troops were very much occupied learning their drill, patrolling the Union Pacific Railroad and protecting the far-flung settlements.

The winter of 1867-68 found the regiment engaged in General Sheridan's winter campaign against Black Kettle's band of Cheyennes. This tribe bore one of the worst reputations of any of the plains Indians They were not confined to reservations, but came in to designated agencies to draw rations, blankets and other supplies Black Kettle was a wily chief, and much hard riding and scouting was required before his band was broken up and their capacity to commit depredations ruined This winter campaign taught them that the troopers could and would follow them to any length, and the Tenth Cavalry did an equal share in wiping out their menace. In one march the regiment was caught in a terrible blizzard and lost over a hundred horses through starvation and freezing

In the fall of 1868 actual service was seen again Company I fought a drawn battle with one hundred Cheyennes at Big Sandy Creek on September 15th, losing ten horses, but killing seven hostiles

In the same month Companies H and I formed part of the relief party to the rescue of Lieutenant Colonel George A Forsyth, who, with a party of scouts, was attacked and "corralled" by a force of about 700 Indians on an island in the Republican River Two of Forsyth's scouts stole through the Indian lines and brought word of the perilous situation of the command to Fort Wallace Parties were soon on the way to its relief First and last the following troops were started toward it from different points · Captain Bankhead with about one hundred men of the 5th Infantry, Captain Carpenter with Co H, Captain Graham with Co. I of the 10th Cavalry, and two companies of the 2nd Cavalry under Major Brisbin

Captain Carpenter's company was the first of these commands to arrive upon the scene It found Forsyth's command out of rations, living on horse flesh without salt or pepper All its officers had been killed or wounded Every horse and mule, too, had been killed Forsyth, who had been twice wounded, was lying in a square hole scooped out in the sand within a few feet of the line of dead horses which half encircled the hole and impregnated the air with a terrible stench Captain Carpenter immediately pitched a number of tents in a suitable place nearby, had the wounded men carried to them, and the rest removed to a more salubrious air

Twenty-six hours later Captain Bankhead arrived bringing with him the companies of the 2nd Cavalry

On October 14th, 1868, two weeks after he had returned to Fort Wallace with the wounded of Forsyth's command, Captain Carpenter was ordered to take his own company, H, and Co I of the 10th Cavalry, and escort Major Carr, of the 5th Cavalry to his command, supposed to be on Beaver Creek On the march he was attacked by a force of about five hundred Indians After proceeding, regardless of the enemy's firing and yelling, far enough to gain a suitable position, he halted his command, had the wagons corralled close together and rushed his men inside at a gallop He had them dismount, tie their horses to the wagons, and form on the outside around the corral Then followed a volley of Spencers which drove the Indians back as though they were thrown from a cannon

A number of the warriors, showing more bravery than the others, undertook to stand their ground. Nearly all of these, together with their ponies, were killed Three dead warriors lay within fifty yards of the wagons The Indians were so demoralized by these results that they did not renew the attack and the troops accomplished their march without further molestation They were back at Fort Wallace on the 21st, having traveled 230 miles in about seven days

For their gallantry in the fight, which took place on Beaver Creek, the officers and men were thanked by General Sheridan in a general field order; Captain Carpenter was breveted Colonel and awarded a Medal of Honor

BENJAMIN H. GRIERSON
THE REGIMENT'S FIRST COLONEL

In April, 1869, headquarters and troops moved to Camp Wichita, in Indian Territory. Camp Wichita was established on the flat directly northeast of the site selected for the post, on the bank of the Medicine Bluff Creek near its junction with Cache Creek.

The only shelter they had was the tentage which they brought with them, much of which had been condemned. An old saw mill was moved up from Fort Arbuckle, fatigue parties were detailed to cut logs in the Wichita Mountains west of the camp, rock quarries were opened in the vicinity and the erection of temporary shelter for men and animals commenced. These were "jackal" buildings with mud roofs and floors.

Very few of the recruits assigned to the regiment could read or write, many of them being plantation hands from the South. Seldom could one be found capable of clerical duty, so that the officers were obliged to do most of their paper work. Quite a number of the recruits had served in the colored regiments during the Civil War, and these furnished the non-commissioned officers. On the whole the men were obedient, amenable to discipline and anxious to learn, besides being proud of their uniform

Even the band was organized, not from musicians, but by selecting men who could read and write and teaching them music. General Grierson, who was himself an accomplished musician, gave them his personal attention and soon succeeded in having a competent leader enlisted and assigned to the regiment

With this handicap in the way of skilled men, the erection of the permanent post was commenced, principally with the labor of the troops. The government was very penurious in the matter of furnishing skilled labor and material. Very few skilled mechanics were allowed and these only for superintendents and overseers. The soldiers ran the saw mill, quarried rock, burned lime and dressed and laid the stone in the walls. In this way a post for ten troops of cavalry, officers' quarters, barracks, stables and storehouses were built

In the summer of 1872, General Sherman, then in command of the Army, made a tour of inspection of the posts in the Department of Texas. When between Forts Griffin and Richardson they met a contractor's mule train hauling supplies to Fort Griffin. Soon after General Sherman and his party arrived at Fort Richardson a teamster from this train arrived at the post with information that the train had been captured by a party of Indians, the teamsters, except this one, who had escaped, were killed, the wagons burned and the mules driven off. The General and his party continued their journey to Fort Sill. The day after their arrival, being ration day, the Kiowas and Comanches in large numbers, probably seven or eight thousand, men, women and children came into the agency, which was on the military reservation about half a mile from the post. "Satanta," a chief of the Kiowas, openly boasted that he was the leader of the band which had captured the train. The Indian agent sent a note to the post commander requesting that he be arrested, also "Satank," another influential chief, and a young Indian named "Big Tree." In the meantime, Satanta and Satank came into the post to see the "Big Chief," who, they learned, was at the commanding officer's house

The troops had orders to "saddle up" and remain in the stables where they could not be seen. While the conversation between General Sherman and the two chiefs was being conducted on the commanding officer's portico, "Big Tree" rode by on his way to the trader's store. The adjutant was directed to take a detachment and arrest him. He was found in the rear of the store, and upon seeing the guard pulled his blanket about his head and jumped through a window, carrying sash and glass with him, vaulted over a high stockade fence and ran like a deer through the troop gardens toward a thicket. The guard fired several shots at him, and the adjutant (Lt Woodward) mounted, pursued and caught him just as he was about to enter the thicket, bound him with a lariat and took him to the commanding officer's quarters. In anticipation of the final decision to confine Satanta and Satank, a dismounted detachment had been secretly sent, one by one, to enter the commanding officer's house by the rear and was concealed in a front room ready for an emergency. When the general indicated that he wished them arrested, the guard filed out and surrounded the porch. At this juncture, Lone Wolf, a vicious and desperate Kiowa chief, rode up, dismounted and came on the porch, smiling and ejaculating the familiar Indian greeting "How, How," threw aside his blanket and disclosed two loaded carbines, one of which he passed to another Indian. With an almost superhuman effort, General

Grierson sprang upon the two Indians, seized the muzzles of the carbines, and sat both Indians squat upon the porch floor. The guard levelled their carbines, but General Grierson's action prevented what, for a moment, threatened a serious tragedy.

Indians were passing through the post and exhibited much excitement. As a precaution, a small detaching of mounted troops was placed at each of the four corners of the parade. Some Indians riding into the post from the southeast, perceiving the commotion on the porch, fired upon one detachment, wounding a horse, and fled. This detachment pursued and fired upon them and killed one, his companion closing in on him and carrying him off mounted. The firing was heard by the Indians at the agency and a wild stampede occurred.

Satanta, Satank and Big Tree were confined in the guard house and a short time afterwards were turned over to General MacKenzie, colonel of the Fourth Cavalry who came through the post with a detachment of his regiment, with orders to turn them over to the civil authorities of Texas to be tried for murder. As the three Indians were brought from the guard house to be put in a wagon, Satank started a weird chant, which we afterwards learned was his "death song." No one understood him except the other two Indians, who, fearing the consequences of an outbreak by him, caught him and put him forcibly into a wagon, taking the precaution to get in another wagon themselves. In the wagon with Satank was a soldier of the Fourth Cavalry who was unable to ride his horse. A short distance from the post, Satank, who had concealed a knife about his person, attacked and stabbed the soldier and seized his carbine, which was loaded. The soldier rolled out of the wagon, and the Indian attempted to fire on the guard which surrounded the wagon, but a shot broke his wrist and others soon ended his earthly career.

During the seven years the regiment was at Fort Sill, besides watching and controlling the Indians, it was largely engaged in suppressing horse and cattle thieves, and whiskey peddlers.

After establishing and building a post there, this camp was named Fort Sill. Life at Sill was not a picnic. More than once the garrison stood to arms in apprehension of an attack. Scouting parties were continually in the field running down marauders, desperadoes, outlaws, hostiles on the war path, and many times only a demonstration in force succeeded in keeping the Red Men within their bounds.

An example of the manifold duties falling to the troops during this period, is the entry in the regimental return. "Company D—February 25th. Left Fort Arbuckle for Cottonwood Grove to assist Indian agent in reclaiming white children held captives by Indians."

On the 11th of June, 1871, Camp Supply was charged by a horde of Comanches, who endeavored to pursue their favorite tactics of stampeding the horses and stock. The Indians were promptly driven off and pursued by Companies A, F, H, I, K, and three companies of the Third Infantry. In the fight that ensued three soldiers were wounded and several horses killed. The Indians lost six killed and ten wounded.

It was about this time that the colored troopers became known among the Indians as the "Buffalo Soldiers." Years later, when a design for the regimental coat of arms was being prepared, the buffalo was adopted as a crest. The Indians of that day learned a wholesome respect for the tireless troopers who, once on the trail, could not be shaken off.

Among the stations garrisoned by the regiment in this period were Forts Dodge, Gibson and Arbuckle, Camp Supply and the Cheyenne agency, in the Indian Territory.

A pitched battle was staged in August, 1874, between the hostiles and the defenders of the Wichita agency. The Kiowas and Naconees strongly resented the establishment of the post, and had planned a coup to wipe out the settlers, soldiers and every building. The hostiles numbered some five hundred. Companies C, E, H and L of the Tenth Cavalry comprised the garrison.

The attack was launched from all sides by the determined Red Men. The surrounding prairie was fired at many points, with the purpose of burning the defenders out, stampeding horses, and burning the buildings. The soldiers had their hands full fighting the fires and repulsing the repeated attacks by the encircling Indians, which were delivered with great courage. Affairs were about to become serious, when Captain Carpenter mounted his company (H) and charged through their center. This charge broke the spirit of the attackers, who fell back in confusion, leaving on the field a large amount of booty.

In April, 1873, a part of the regiment made the acquaintance of Texas. Companies E, I and L were stationed at Fort Richardson, C at Fort Griffin, F at Fort Concho. Headquarters remained at Fort Sill until March, 1875. The troops remaining in Indian Territory took part in the campaign of 1874-75 against the Kiowas and Comanches. In this campaign, Companies D and M, with one company of the Eleventh Infantry, commanded by Major Schofield, captured a band of more than 300 hostiles and 1500 ponies at Elk Creek, Indian Territory, October 25, 1874.

Among the prisoners were a number of irreconcilables—"bad Injuns." These were closely confined at Fort Sill and later transferred to Fort Marion in far off Florida, for restriction. Captain Pratt went in charge of this party, and never rejoined the regiment. He was a fine officer and very sympathetic towards the Indians. As Superintendent of the Carlisle Indian School he gained wide fame.

On the 6th of April, 1875, occurred the chase after Black Horse's band. He was at the Cheyenne agency awaiting transportation to Fort Marion. Knocking down his guard, he escaped and ran for the camp of his tribe nearby. He was killed as he ran by Captain Bennett, Fifth Infantry. This was the signal for an exodus. Practically the whole tribe abandoned camp that night and took to the hills, but not before engaging in a brisk skirmish with Companies D and M, in which one soldier was killed and twelve wounded. The Indians lost eight killed. Tenth Cavalry marksmanship was improving with practice. After a ten day chase most of the Indians returned to the agency.

Headquarters was established at Fort Concho, Texas, on April 17, 1875. The May return shows the troops stationed as follows.

Companies A, D, F, G, I and L at Fort Concho
Companies B and E at Fort Griffin
Companies C and K at Fort McKavett
Company H at Fort Davis
Company M at Fort Stockton

In the next seven years that headquarters remained at Fort Concho, the troops were scattered all over west Texas, as occasion demanded, and added to their reputation as Indian fighters when they met the Apaches. Their work was a long succession of hikes and pursuits, with now and then a consoling skirmish with Indians or desperadoes. Their trails led them far into Mexico, into and over the grim fastness of the Guadalupe Mountains, across the deserts of the Staked Plains, the Bad Lands of the Rio Grande and the Big Bend.

Regard a few bald entries in the regimental returns of 1876 and 1877, picked at random.

1876

"Co C—Fort McKavett, Texas

The company returned from scout duty in field against hostiles after absence of six months and seven days"

"Co G—Fort Griffin, Texas

Corporal John Robinson and four men pursued Mexican horse thieves, returned November 28, 1876, captured 10 Mexicans, 15 horses Distance marched 770 miles"

1877

"Co A—

Private Derwin died July 30th from want of water Private Gordon died July 31st, being without water for 86 hours Privates Bond and Isaacs missing since July 30th on account of straggling."

"Headquarters—

"1st Lt R G Smither, Adjutant, with effective force of band, (16 men) started on scout August 3rd to Bull Creek, Texas, distance of 140 miles, in 41 hours, for relief of Captain Nolan's command which was reported in suffering condition on Staked Plains Men and horses dying from lack of water Returned to Fort Concho August 14th"

"Co F—Camp on the Rio Grande, Texas.

Since last report the company has been engaged in scouting after hostile Indians Distance marched 1500 miles"

"Co G—May 4th, Fort Griffin, Texas

Captain Lee, Lieut Jones, and 42 men, left post April 9, 1877, in pursuit hostile Indians Surprised Comanche village at Lake Quemado, Texas, killed four Indians, captured six squaws, and 69 horses 1st Sergeant Charles Baker killed in action - Distance marched 750 miles"

"Co I—Fort Richardson, Texas

2d Lieutenant Jewett and 24 enlisted men returned from a scout on the Staked Plains One public horse, Captain Baldwin responsible, died on Staked Plains October 25th Distance marched 1360 miles"

Those were the days that tried men's souls, and welded the organizations into bands of true and tried veterans Captain Bourke of the Third Cavalry, has written of those days

"To march into battle with banners flying, drums beating, and the pulse throbbing high with the promptings of honorable ambition and enthusiasm, in unison with the roar of artillery, does not call for half the nerve and determination that must be daily exercised to pursue, mile after mile, in such terrible weather, over rugged mountains and through unknown cañons, a foe whose habits of warfare are repugnant to every principle of humanity, and whose presence can be determined solely by the flash of the rifle which lays some poor sentry low, or the whoop and yell which stampeded our stock from the grazing grounds. The life of a soldier, in time of war, has scarcely a compensating feature, but he ordinarily expects palatable food whenever obtainable, and good, warm quarters during the winter season In campaigning against the Indians, if anxious to gain success, he must lay aside every idea of good food and comfortable lodgings, and make up his mind to undergo with cheerfulness privations from which other soldiers would shrink back dismayed. His sole object should be to strike the enemy and to strike him hard, and this accomplished should be full compensation for all privations undergone With all its disadvantages this system of Indian warfare is a grand school for the cavalrymen of the future, teaching them fortitude, vigilance, self-reliance, and dexterity, besides that instruction in handling, marching, feeding, and fighting troops which no school can impart in text-books."

The frontier was an imaginary line when pursuing marauders. A picked detachment of Company B, under Lieut. Evans, and two Seminole scouts, surprised a camp of the Lipans and Kickapoos near Saragossa, Mexico, on July 30, 1876, after a forced march of 110 miles in twenty-five hours. Ten Indians were killed, 93 captured, with the loss of one horse. Twenty-three lodges were destroyed. Captain Lebo also led Companies B, E and K into the Pinto Mountains of Mexico and destroyed a village on August 12, 1876.

The Victoria campaign of 1880 resulted in the breaking up of that wily chieftain's band, teaching it such a lesson that he never again came north of the Rio Grande.

In July of that year, Victoria and all his band broke out from the Mescalero reservation in New Mexico and started through Texas on a reign of terror, murder and pillage.

Colonel Grierson, on a scout with only six men, was attacked by this band near Eagle Springs, and was barely rescued by a reinforcement from Company C, of Lieut. Finley with 15 men. Later, Companies A and C came up, driving the Apaches off after a four-hour fight. The pursuit was carried to the Rio Grande.

The bad reputation these Apaches bore did not feaze the troopers of the Tenth Cavalry. A detachment from Company H, under Corporal Asa Weaver, out on patrol, did not hesitate to head off the band in its retreat after it had crossed the river into Mexico, but joined in a running fight of 15 miles. Near El Alamo, the horse of Private Tockes became unmanageable, being wounded with an arrow. It bucked and stampeded into the midst of the Indian rear guard. When last seen, this brave man was discerned to have dropped his reins, drawn his carbine, and was selling his life dearly. Months later his skeleton was found.

Corporal Weaver was promoted on the spot to a sergeantcy for his gallantry and qualities of leadership.

Colonel Grierson personally led the column that, by a forced march of 65 miles, intercepted Victoria's retreat and forced him to cross into Mexico, whence he never returned to raid. He was later killed by Mexican soldiery near Lake Guzman.

Under the "Record of Events," the following are typical:

"Co K—Sculptured Tanks, Guadalupe Mountains, N. M., April, 1880.

Left Salada Water Holes, Texas, April 1st, arrived at Black River Falls, N. M. Marched thence northward through the Guadalupe Mountains by way of Guadalupe Creek to the Rio Panasco in the Sacramento Mountains, thence to the agency and took part in the disarming and dismounting the Mescalero Indians. April 9th struck the camp of a small party of Mescaleros at Shakehand Springs, N. M. Killed one buck, captured four squaws and one child, released from captivity a small Mexican boy (Cayetana Segura) aged 11. Captured 21 head of horses and mules, and destroyed their camp. Distance marched, 417½ miles."

"Company A—Near old Fort Quitman, Texas, August, 1880.

Left Eagle Springs, Texas, August 2nd and marched to Van Horn's Wells. August 3rd, marched to Devil's Race Course. August 4th, marched to Rattle Snake Springs, 6th, 7th and 8th, engaged in scouting and picketing the passes of the Sierra Diablo. August 10th, marched to Ash Springs. August 11th, discovered and followed trail of Victoria's band of Apaches from 8.00 p. m.

until 11:45 a. m. of the 12th, when, after marching and reaching the Rio Grande, the pursuit ended by reason of the enemy crossing the river into Mexico. Distance marched by company and detachments, 748 miles."

"Company G—Sulphur Water Hole, Texas, August, 1880.

Left Eagle Springs, Texas, August 3rd, arriving at Van Horn, Texas, the same night; August 4th, 5th, marched to Rattle Snake Springs, Texas. August 6th, engaged with hostile Indians near Rattlesnake Springs. No casualties. August 7th, marched to Sulphur Water Hole, Texas. August 3rd, Private Julius London, one of the party of scouts, was engaged and wounded in action with hostile Apaches near Eagle Springs, Texas. Distance marched 1256 miles."

"Company H—Near Hot Springs, Texas, August, 1880.

August 1st, engaged in furnishing pickets and scouts from Eagle Springs, Texas. August 3rd, Corporal A. Weaver, with Pvt. Brent of H Company, and a small detail from other companies, while on picket at Alamo Springs, discovered Victoria's band of Indians after they had crossed the Rio Grande and had an engagement and running fight for 15 miles. August 3rd, left Eagle Springs in pursuit of Victoria's band. Marched to Van Horn and thence to Devil's Race Course, thence across to the Rattle Snake Springs. August 6th, participated in an engagement with Victoria's band with Companies B, C and G, under command of Capt. L. H. Carpenter, the Indians being repulsed and fleeing to the mountains. Pvt. Wesley Hardy missing in action. Distance marched by company and detachments, 1250 miles."

On January 1, 1881, the designation was changed from "Company" to "Troop."

Regimental headquarters moved to Fort Davis in July, 1882, and remained until March, 1885. In these three years the troops performed the same old dismal frontier service, with few comforts, and no luxuries. But they were close to being a perfect cavalry fighting machine; they were lean and hard and grizzled, and loved a fight. This entry appears in Troop M's records:

"Jan., '84, Piña-Colorado, Texas. Saddler Ross mortally wounded. Sgt. Winfield Scott and Pvt. Augustus Dover slightly wounded, while arresting a desperado on the military reservation. The desperado, W. A. Alexander, was killed while resisting arrest."

Chapter III
THE BUFFALO SOLDIERS IN ARIZONA

IN THE Spring of 1885, the regiment moved westward into the Department of Arizona, where the Apaches held sway. Geronimo, the Kid, Mangus, Cochise, Alchise, Aklenni, Natsin, Eskiltie and other chieftains had dotted the plains and cañons of Arizona with the graves of thousands of emigrants, settlers and prospectors. The department was commanded by that famous Indian fighter and administrator, General Crook.

Marching along the Southern Pacific Railroad, the column was joined at Camp Rice by Troop I. For the first time in its history the regiment was gathered together. The twelve troops, headquarters and band, continued together to Bowie Station, Arizona, in the Chiricahua Mountains. Here the troops again separated to go to their posts, as follows:

Headquarters and Troop B, Whipple Barracks; A, Fort Apache; C, F and G, Fort Thomas; D, E, H, K and L, Fort Grant; I and M, Fort Verde. Lieut. Colonel Wade took station at Apache; Major Mills at Thomas; Major McClellan at Verde, and Major Van Vliet at Grant. The chaplain held out at Apache.

The Geronimo campaign was under way, and immediately a squadron composed of Troops D, E, H and K was put in the field under Major Van Vliet. They ransacked every trail in the Mogollon Mountains, even as far as Fort Bayard, New Mexico, but were evidently on the wrong trail. All the troops of the regiment were in the field in this campaign.

Several officers used pull and had themselves detailed with the Indian scouts, hoping in that way to get to the front of the front. Lieut. Shipp was thus with Captain Crawford in his tragic expedition way down in Mexico. Lieut. Finley accompanied Captain Lawton Fourth Cavalry, when he forced the surrender of Geronimo and his band.

The second Medal of Honor in the regiment was won by Lieut. Powhatan H. Clarke, who had accompanied Captain Lebo's troop (K) from Calabasas into Mexico. On May 3rd, 1886, the troop, after a remarkable march of over two hundred miles, came up with Geronimo's band in the Pinito Mountains. The fighting was of a most desperate character; the Indians were in their own chosen positions, in gorges and on inaccessible cliffs. Corporal Scott was wounded seriously, and lying exposed to the enemy's fire. Lieut. Clarke ran, without hesitation, to his aid, picked him up and carried him to safety through a hail of missiles.

In October, Chief Mangus and his band were run down by Troop H in the White Mountains, east of Fort Apache, after a running fight of 45 miles over almost impassable country. Captain Cooper then had H Troop

LIEUT. POWHATAN H. CLARKE WINNING MEDAL OF HONOR
(FROM PAINTING PRESENTED BY THE ARTIST, T. HOLROYD LAMBERT)

CAPTAIN T. C. LEBO

For most of the troops there was little glory in this campaign. Their's was the harder duty, to prevent outbreaks, rather than chase the renegades back onto their reservations. Their's was the dismal duty to guard mountain passes, water holes, and trails that did not lead to glorious fighting.

In 1887, about half the regiment pursued the "Kid," one of Geronimo's disciples. It was a hard campaign, but unsuccessful. He was never caught; he may still be running. Lieut. Carter P. Johnson gained commendation by the skill, energy and endurance with which his outfit pursued this outlaw.

Headquarters move to Fort Grant in July, 1886, thence to Santa Fe, New Mexico, in November of the same year.

The following order was published to the troops in Arizona:

"HEADQUARTERS DEPARTMENT OF ARIZONA,
"Willcox, A T, October 7, 1886
"General Field Orders No 12

'It is gratifying to the Commanding General to announce to the troops serving in this Department the close of the Indian campaign, and the establishment of permanent peace and security against future depredations of the hostile Apaches, as the result of the fortitude and endurance of the troops in the field

"You have effected the subjugation of the hostiles under Geronimo and Natchez, and, with the exception of one small thieving party now in Chihuahua, Mexico, all have been removed to a place of safe custody. At the same time the entire tribe of Chiricahua and Warm Springs Indians, whose presence has been a menace to the settlements and whose camps have for years been the rendezvous, the source of supplies, and the safe refuge of the hostile element, have been entirely removed from these territories

For centuries the warlike Apaches have been a terror to this country Neither Indian nor Spaniard have been able to successfully cope with them in their peculiar methods of savage warfare, and for years they have retarded the progress of civilization and industry It was against such an enemy as this, and in a wild, arid country, traversed by a series of rugged and almost impassable mountain ranges, with great scarcity of water, that the troops, already worn and tried, re-entered the field

"In the early days of April last, the hostiles, then in Sonora, Mexico, began their depredations, and on the 27th of that month invaded the territory of Arizona They at once met active opposition, Captain T C Lebo, Tenth Cavalry, true to his reputation as a gallant and successful cavalry leader, moving first against them He followed the hostiles rapidly for over two hundred miles, and finally, on May 3rd, forced them to an encounter During this spirited engagement the officers and men evinced great bravery, contending against an enemy on ground of their own choosing, among rugged cliffs almost inaccessible During the engagement, Corporal Scott, a brave soldier, lay disabled with a serious wound, exposed to the enemy's fire, and Lieut P H Clarke, Tenth Cavalry, rushed to his assistance, carrying him to a place of safety Such acts of heroism are worthy of great praise After the engagement the hostiles continued their flight, and for nearly a fortnight the troops, under Lieut Benson, Captains Lebo and Lawton, continued the pursuit without cessation. * * *

"* * * Subsequently the trail of the hostiles was taken up by several other detachments acting in concert, each commanded by energetic and capable officers, until Captain J T Morrison, Tenth Cavalry, near Fort Apache, captured all their horses, and they took flight on foot south and were driven across the Mexican boundary The other band, meanwhile, had been pursued by other commands through the Santa Rita, Whetstone, Santa Catalina and Rincon Mountains, and on the evening of June 5th, when in the Patagonia Mountains, were surrounded and much of their stock and equipment captured by Lieut R D Wash, Fourth Cavalry

"* * * The march of Lebo's troop, 20 miles in two hours; Benson's ride of 90 miles in 19 hours, and Dr Wood's* skill and remarkable marches with a detachment of infantry, are worthy of mention

* * * Now that all has been accomplished, the troops in this Department will duly appreciate the feeling of relief as expressed by the people of Sonora, Mexico, through their governor, Louis E Torres, the resolution of thanks for your heroic services offered by all parties in every section of Arizona and New Mexico, the approval of General Sheridan and Secretary Endicott, all of which are most gratifying, but you will regard higher than all praise, the deep and lasting gratitude which comes from the thousands of homes scattered over this vast area to which you have given security and happiness

"By command of Brigadier General Miles

"WM A THOMPSON,
"Captain Fourth Cavalry, A A A. G.

"OFFICIAL.
"G B RUSSELL,
"Acting Assistant Adjutant General"

---

*Now Major General Leonard Wood —(Editor)

The regiment was now to lose its colonel, who relieved General Nelson A Miles in command of the Department of Arizona His last official act was a farewell to the regiment

"HEADQUARTERS TENTH CAVALRY,
Santa Fe, New Mexico, December 1st, 1888

"Orders No 51

'In pursuance of General Orders No 97, current series, Headquarters of the Army, announcing his assignment to the command of the Department of Arizona, the undersigned relinquishes command of the Tenth U S Cavalry.

'In doing so he desires to express his deep regret at being thus separated from the regiment he organized and has so long commanded, but he is gratified to be able, at this time, to refer, even briefly, to its splendid record of nearly twenty-two years service to the Government, while under his command, rendered, as it has been, in the field and at the most isolated posts on the frontier, always in the vanguard of civilization and in contact with the most warlike and savage Indians of the plains

"The officers and enlisted men have cheerfully endured many hardships and privations, and in the midst of great dangers steadfastly maintained a most gallant and zealous devotion to duty, and they may well be proud of the record made, and rest assured that the hard work undergone in the accomplishment of such important and valuable service to their country, is well understood and appreciated, and that it cannot fail, sooner or later, to meet with due recognition and reward

'That the high standard of excellence gained by the regiment for discipline and efficiency in the past will be fully sustained in the future, that the most signal success will ever attend the officers and soldiers of the Tenth Cavalry in all their noble efforts and undertakings, official or otherwise, is the heartfelt wish of their old commander

(Signed) "BENJAMIN H GRIERSON,
"Colonel Tenth U S Cavalry, Brevet Major-General"

Colonel Grierson was promoted to Brigadier in April, 1890, and retired July 8, in the same year, dearly beloved by every man in the regiment

Colonel J K Mizner was next assigned to command, and joined in August, 1890, at Fort Apache. Lieut Colonel George C Hunt was commanding in the meanwhile The field and staff then comprised in addition: Majors C B McClellan, Van Vliet and Norvell, 1st Lieut T W Jones, Adjutant, 1st Lieut L Finley, Quartermaster, F H Weaver, Chaplain

The Indians were by now fairly well settled down to farming on their reservations, and except for sporadic outbreaks by a few of the worst, there was little field service Lieut Clarke, with a detachment of picked men and scouts, had a roving commission to run down the few hostiles still 'out," and did excellent work

In 1891 there were two expeditions sent into the Moki country General Corbin accompanied the latter expedition of Troops B and E

Colonel Mizner wrote to the Adjutant General in August, 1891, drawing attention to the fact that for twenty consecutive years the Tenth Cavalry had served south of the 36th latitude, in the most undesirable stations known to any branch of the service, and with fewer accommodations as to quarters or barracks, and requested a gradual change to a northern climate, preferably not further than Kansas With characteristic kindness, orders came to move at once to Montana, detraining there in midwinter, in a blizzard The regiment left Arizona in the southern spring

Relieving the First Cavalry, the Tenth Cavalry took over their horses, troop for troop Troop A of the First was in Virginia, so to mount our own A troop, Montana horses were secured, brand new to military service The regiment took stations in the Department of Dakota as follows

COLONEL J. K. MIZNER

Headquarters and Band, Fort Custer, Montana.
Troop A, Fort Custer, Montana.
Troop B, Fort Custer, Montana.
Troop C, Fort Assinniboine, Montana.
Troop D, Fort Keogh, Montana.
Troop E, Fort Custer, Montana.
Troop F, Fort Assinniboine, Montana.
Troop G, Fort Custer, Montana.
Troop H, Fort Buford, North Dakota.
Troop I, Fort Leavenworth, Kansas.
Troop K, Fort Custer, Montana.

Troops L and M, which were skeletonized, were considered at headquarters.

Life in Montana and North Dakota was a great relaxation for our veterans after their strenuous work in Arizona. They enjoyed the hunting and change of scenery and became acquainted with the country, making long practice marches, sometimes in the dead of winter, through blizzards. Forts Keogh and Buford earned the reputation of being the coldest stations in the country.

The regiment lost Lieut. Clarke, who was drowned in the Little Big Horn River on July 21, 1893. His death was keenly felt by his comrades. In February, 1894, Lieut.

Finley was injured at drill when his horse fell and crushed his leg. He failed to recover from the amputation; thus in less than a year two well loved officers came to an untimely end.

Troops B, L, G and K had some relaxation when they were called out in April, 1894, to suppress a part of "Coxey's Commonwealers." These had held up a Northern Pacific train and were generally obnoxious. Parts of the regiment were called out this summer on strike duty to protect the railroad from strikers.

Headquarters moved to Fort Assinniboine November 20, 1894.

Troop I mourned the loss of First Sergeant James Brown, who was frozen to death in a blizzard February 5, 1895. One of the best types of old soldier, his death was grieved throughout the regiment.

In the summer of 1896 the whole regiment was in the field rounding up Cree Indians, who were still off their reservations in Canada, and had been stealing and committing minor depredations since 1877. Great bands of Indians were gathered in and turned over to the Canadians at the border. Lieut. Pershing, commanding Troop D, was out all summer, marching over 600 miles.

Colonel Mizner was promoted to be Brigadier General in June, 1897. His farewell to the regiment is expressed in the following:

"HEADQUARTERS TENTH U S CAVALRY,
"Fort Assinibome, Montana, June 7th, 1897
"General Orders No 1

'The President having been pleased to advance the undersigned to the grade of Brigadier General, he hereby relinquishes command of the Tenth Cavalry and of the post of Fort Assinniboine, Montana.

"In severing his connection with the Tenth U. S. Cavalry, of which he has been Colonel for more than seven years it affords him unbounded pleasure to commend both officers and men for their loyalty to their country and for their devotion to every duty, however trying and arduous.

"For efficiency and discipline and valuable service the regiment has a history of which it may justly be proud.

"With a sense of deep obligation to the officers for their zealous support and generous courtesies and high appreciation of the excellent soldierly conduct and good behavior of the men, he wishes for each a prosperous and happy future and bids them all farewell.
(Signed) J K MIZNER,
"Brigadier General, U S Army"

Lieut Colonel Baldwin commanded until the arrival of Colonel Guy V. Henry on October 29, 1897.

During this summer, Troops A, E and K were called out under Major Norvell to arrest several 'bad Injuns" near the Tongue River Agency. Trouble was anticipated in arresting the bucks, "Whirlwind," "Shoulder Blade," "Yellow Hair," and 'Sam Crow," on account of the attitude of the rest of the Cneyenne tribe. However, owing to the skill and diplomacy of Major Norvell and Captain Read, and not a little to the respect of the Cheyennes for their old friends the "Buffalo Soldiers," the arrests were made without untoward incident, and the troops were recalled.

The War Department saw fit to order the abandonment of Fort Custer this winter (1897) and the garrison moved to other posts. The change was made in December, with the thermometer flirting around the 40° mark below zero.

January 1st, 1898, found the regiment assembled at Fort Assinniboine, less Troops A, B and E, at Fort Keogh, Montana.

CHAPTER IV.
CUBA AND THE PHILIPPINES
1898-1902

THE destruction of the Maine in Havana Harbor raised the excitement in the regiment to fever pitch. The big chance to show its real mettle had come, and every man was ready and eager for the test of battle, and for the opportunity to fight shoulder to shoulder alongside the white regiments. Every officer felt confident of his men, and anxious to put them in the "Big Show."

Orders to concentrate at Chickamauga Park, Georgia, were received in the middle of April. On April 25th, the regiment was camped in Dyer's Field, near the position made famous by General Thomas' stand at the Battle Above the Clouds, where he earned the appellation of the "Rock of Chickamauga."

Busy days followed, drills and more drills. The skeleton Troops L and M were reorganized by drafts from the other troops. Great was the day when Colonel Henry assembled the officers after a final review and said "They'll do." Colonel Henry became a Brigadier General of Volunteers and was fated never to rejoin the regiment. Lieut. Colonel T. A. Baldwin assumed command.

Marching on May 14th to Rossville, the regiment entrained there for Tampa, but was diverted to Lakeland, arriving there the 16th.

On June 7th, two squadrons left for Tampa: Major Norvell with Troops A, B, E and I; Major Wint with Troops C, D, F and G. It was a trial to have to bid the horses goodbye, but cavalrymen have to show that they can fight as infantry also, and as well as. The feelings of the other troops at having to stay at Lakeland in charge of baggage and horses can be well imagined.

COLONEL GUY V. HENRY

The troops embarked on the S. S. "Leona" with the First Cavalry, with the exception of Troops C and F which sailed on the "Alamo." For seven days the steamers floated at Tampa; travel rations only were furnished.

Joy came to the old soldiers of Troop M, when Lieut. C. P. Johnson was given a detachment from it and from the other outfits at Lakeland; they were to perform a "special mission" in Cuba. Better, they were mounted. With them went General Munez and staff, 375 assorted Cubans, and a great quantity of arms and munitions for General Gomez. They sailed on the Florida, convoyed by the Peoria, on June 21st.

A landing was attempted near Tunas, but the Florida ran aground; Spanish troops rapidly assembled and poured a hot fire on the two ships. The little gunboat Peoria was quite insufficient. Fortunately the larger gunboat Helena came along, towed the Florida off the sandbar, and gave the Spaniards a few whiffs of shrapnel. The landing was effected at Palo Alto, and made a junction with General Gomez July 3rd. The records cast little light on the doings of this detachment, but they "cooperated" with the Cubans, without casualties, and the M troopers rejoined the regiment at Montauk in September.

To go back to our two squadrons:

Disembarkation was effected at Daiquiri on June 22nd by Major Norvell's squadron, and on the 23rd by Major Wint's. The first deaths of the campaign resulted from the overturning of a boat. Corporal Edward T. Cobb and Private George English, of B Troop, were unable to swim, and were drowned.

Always in the van, Major Norvell's squadron was part of the first column towards Siboney, which comprised in addition one squadron of the First Cavalry, and two squadrons of the Rough Riders Captain Watson, Tenth Cavalry, commanded the four Hotchkiss guns that went along with this column

The next day (24th) this force was ordered by General Wheeler to take the heights of Las Guasimas, strongly held by the Spaniards Contact was made at 7 30 a m, when volleys were fired from the heights The Rough Riders were on the left flank of the advance Deployment was difficult owing to the high jungle-like grass and vegetation. There was difficulty in maintaining any kind of skirmish line The men needed no leading, however They could tell where the Spaniards were from the direction of the firing, and they crawled in that direction individually The defenders had a great advantage through the use of smokeless powder and their naturally strong position was strengthened by a rock wall erected on the crest

The First and Tenth moved up the hill side by side, while the Routh Riders attacked the right flank With a rush the top was gained and only dead and dying Spaniards were seen The rest had "fled precipitately towards Santiago." Corporal George Smith of I Troop, now Master Sergeant of the regiment, was the first man on the crest, and followed immediately by Farrier Sherman Harris, same troop

Major Norvell's squadron, 220 strong, lost in this engagement one corporal killed and seven men wounded (See reports of Major Norvel and those of troop commanders, in Appendix 'B") Lieut Vidmer, Corporal Johnson, Privates Neal, Nelson, Wally, White, Jones, Farrier Harris and Wagoner Boland won commendations for conspicuous bravery in this action

Victory perched on the colors of the Tenth in its first real modern battle

Comparative strength of forces engaged
American, 964   Spanish, 1500

The rest of the brigade came up too late for participation in this engagement Camp was made on the battlefield until the 26th, when the troops moved to Seville, in the direction of Santiago On the 30th of June the brigade arrived at El Poso, just outside of the fortifications of Santiago.

Between El Poso and Santiago lay the San Juan range of hills elevated about one hundred and twenty-five feet with the San Juan River at its eastern base, flowing southward The summit of Little San Juan Hill, or Kettle Hill, is about one-half mile from the highest point of San Juan Hill, and separated from it by an oval lake about three hundred yards long The approach to the San Juan River from El Poso was through the densest varieties of vegetation, cactus and prickly grass. The slopes of the hills were quite barren all the way to the river

The advance against Santiago started early on the morning of July 1st Grimes's battery opened the ball by a bombardment of the enemy's entrenchments and block-houses Lawton's brigade was attacking from the direction of El Caney, and the Second Cavalry brigade was to attack in conjunction, linking up with its left While waiting orders to attack, an observation balloon of the Signal Corps was towed down the road to the assembly point of the brigade, 50 feet above the men of the First and Tenth Cavalry, lying beneath This immediately drew the fire of every Spaniard, no matter what his armament Naturally the casualties beneath the balloon were great It is unfortunate there are no phonographic records of the comments of the troopers suffering beneath it Fortunately, and to their great delight, it was shot down, after affording a thrilling experience to its occupant, Lieut Colonel Derby He was unhurt, except as to his feelings

The infantry regiments on the brigade's left were having a terrible time advancing in the face of the converging fire from Kettle and San Juan Hills. Urgent orders came from General McClernand "to take Kettle Hill at all costs." The job given to the First, Ninth, Tenth and Rough Rider Cavalry was a tough one.

The famous little red-roofed house on the summit was indicated as the objective, and the troops started, waded through the San Juan River, and crawling, running, stumbling, crossed the bare ground up the slope of the hill in the terrific heat, all in the face of a galling fire from the entrenchments on the crest. Reaching the objective, the Spaniards were seen fleeing to safety into the trenches beyond, on San Juan Hill.

The regiment formed in two lines, Troops A, B, E and I in front, led by Major Norvell. Troops C, F and G were in the second line, under Major Wint. Troop D, which had forded the river further down stream, was temporarily separated from the squadron.

Nothing could stop the rush of our men. The two lines became merged into one—a line of cheering, yelling heroes whom bullets could not stop.

1st Lieutenants W. H. Shipp and W. E. Smith were killed while leading their men. They had graduated from West Point together, fell at the same time, and were buried in the same grave on San Juan Hill.

Captain A. L. Mills was shot in the head while reforming his men for the second charge. 2nd Lieutenant F. R. McCoy was severely wounded while in the van of his platoon, and was commended for gallantry. First Lieutenant Livermore, same troop, was commended for gallantry in taking No. 1 blockhouse, where he was wounded. Captain Anderson was struck by a shell burst and received two wounds, but continued with his troop. Captain Bigelow was struck three times when only 75 yards from the blockhouse. Lieutenants Roberts, Barnum, Whitehead and Willard also were wounded.

It is not generally known that the colors of the Third Cavalry were planted on the crest of San Juan by a soldier of the Tenth Cavalry. It happened in this manner. About half way up the slope the colors of the Third were seen to stop and fall, the color bearer sinking to the ground, shot through the body; Sergeant George Berry, color bearer of the Tenth, dashed over to where the colors lay, raised them high, and waving both flags, planted them on the crest side by side. This act won for Sergeant Berry high commendation, and is no doubt the only instance in our military history where the colors of one regiment were carried to the final objective by a member of a rival regiment.

Corporal Walker and Pvt. Luschious Smith were with Lieut. Ord of the Sixth Infantry, and were "the head and front of the assault." These troopers were awarded Certificates of Merit for their gallantry on this day. Since Pvt. Smith exchanged the Certificate of Merit for a Distinguished Service Medal he is the only man now in the regiment, excepting Colonel Winans, who wears the D. S. M.

The famous old hill being taken, the regiment in the most advanced position, commenced to dig in, and that night was occupying rifle pits extending some 800 yards to the right of the Santiago road. Repeated counter attacks were made throughout the night, and rifle firing continued all night. Major Wint was severely wounded while encouraging his men during a night counter attack.

The victory was won, but not without its price. Eleven of the twenty-two officers of the regiment were casualties, and 16½ per cent of the enlisted strength. It was a proud day for the regiment.

Sergeant Graham's heroic action was the subject of two letters from commissioned

LT. COL. T. A. BALDWIN

MAJ. S. T. NORVELL

MAJ. THEO. J. WINT

CAPT. C. G. AYRES

officers, recommending him for a Medal of Honor. He was on duty with the Gatling Gun Battery, and performed the hazardous duty of bringing up ammunition across a fire-swept zone. A shell from the enemy's artillery landed near Lieut. Parker. Without hesitation, Sergeant Graham leaped to Lieut. Parker's side and covered his body with his own. Luckily, the shell fragments struck neither. See Appendix "C" for the letters in full.

General Wheeler specially recommended the following men for a Medal of Honor for their gallantry and coolness under fire.

Troop A—
    Corporal John Anderson
    Private R. A. Parker.
Troop C—
    Sergeant Adam Houston
Troop E—
    1st Sergeant Peter McCann
    Sergeant Benjamin Fasit.
    Sergeant O. G. Gaither
    Sergeant William Payne
    Corporal Thomas H. Herbert
Troop I—
    Private Elsie Jones. (Previously recommended)

Many enlisted men of the Ninth and Tenth Cavalry won commendations for gallantry and were commissioned in the Volunteers. Among those were Sergeant Major Edward L. Baker, Q. M. Sergeant Alfred M. Ray, 1st Sergeant William H. Givens, Sergeant Saint Foster, Sergeant John Buck, and Saddler Sergeant Jacob C. Smith.

Lieutenant Pershing, the Regimental Quartermaster rendered valuable service in the hazardous duty of conducting the troops to their sectors of attack and defense, and was commended by Colonel Baldwin.

The reports of Lieut. Colonel Baldwin, Major Norvell and the troop commanders throw most interesting sidelights on the battle. These appear in Appendix "D."

Colonel Leonard Wood in his report on the conduct of the Second Cavalry Brigade wrote:

"That dismounted cavalry should have been able to charge regular infantry in strong position, supported by artillery entanglements and the general lay of the land, seems almost incredible, yet that is exactly what these troops did, passing over a long zone of fire and charging steep hills topped with works and blockhouses. I can only say that their work was superb."

The thin American lines on San Juan Heights was now within cannon shot range of Santiago, but the situation was one that gave our high command grave anxiety. General Wheeler was the recipient of unsolicited advice to withdraw, as was General Shafer. At 3:00 a. m. of July 2nd, heavy firing broke out, and at 5:30 was general all along the line. Two officers and five men of the Tenth were wounded in this engagement between the trenches; at 10:00 p. m., our men had to beat off a determined attack, supported by artillery. Work on the entrenchments continued without pause, as there was a possibility that the "war of movement" was to degenerate into trench warfare, or a siege.

On July 2nd, in the evening, a conference was held between Generals Shafter, Wheeler, Lawton, Kent and Bates, to decide upon a course of action. It developed that the plan of action was to rest on the reply of General Toral to the demand for the surrender of Santiago, sent under flag of truce on July 3rd at noon.

1ST LT. CARTER P. JOHNSON

1ST LT. MALVERN-HILL BARNUM

2ND LT. FRANK R. McCOY

2ND LT. GEORGE VIDMER

July 3rd dawned to the accompaniment of heavy artillery and musketry fire About 9 00 a m, the booming of heavy guns off the Harbor of Santiago told the men in the trenches that Cervera was out," and that our Navy was taking care of the Spanish fleet Hostilities ceased at noon, when the flag of truce went over, but not before two more men of the Tenth had been wounded Bomb-proofs were constructed, and the troops started to prepare for a long stay in their trenches.

At noon of the 4th of July, the truce continuing, the men were assembled to hear General Miles' congratulatory telegram referring to their work of July 1st The bands played, and a real celebration was held, but this party was small compared to the jubilee held next day when the news came of the destruction of the Spanish fleet

The next four days were spent in strengthening the trenches, and speculating on the chances for a renewal of the fight

Firing commenced again at 4 30 p m of the 10th, but died out about 7 15 p m Early next morning the pickets tried to start something, and by 6 00 a m the firing spread all down the line It took forty minutes of frantic bugling to "Cease firing" for the firing to cease A tropical thunderstorm that night added to the general discomfort of the trenches General Miles, riding down the lines, caught one regiment stark naked, while they were drying their clothing on trees and bushes Every man stood at attention while he passed. He said later that it was the strangest review he ever had

Early on the 14th a warning order came to the effect that the attack would be launched at noon In the midse of preparations for it, however, General Toral indicated his surrender, and the chances for another battle were lost

On the 17th the parapets were manned to witness the formal surrender of General Toral at 9 30 a m At noon the Stars and Stripes climbed the flag staff over Santiago, and the campaign was over

The regiment marched to camp grounds at El Caney on the 18th, and remained there until it embarked for Montauk Point, L I on August 13th The trip to Montauk Point required eight days, and then our veterans endured the famous Detention Camp until October 6th, a period of six weeks. The "out of luck' troops at Lakeside, in the meanwhile, had brought up the horses and baggage, so that they could be brought right back to Alabama Anyway, there was a great reunion on the 21st, and much swapping of yarns There was no argument—the Tenth had won the war

The regiment was slated for a temporary stay in Huntsville, Alabama As a special compliment, President McKinley reviewed the regiment in Washington, D C, ordering it detrained for the purpose The President was most complimentary in his remarks to Colonel Baldwin, who agreed with him perfectly

Camp in Huntsville was made October 11th, and our veterans had no trouble making friends and getting married The citizens of this city were most cordial, and their hospitality unbounded.

The band and the two veteran squadrons took part in the Peace Jubilee in Philadelphia in October Here they were presented with a beautiful stand of colors, a gift of the colored citizens of Philadelphia It will be remembered that Philadelphia, twenty-two years previous, had furnished Captain Carpenter the high class recruits who were to become the backbone of the regiment

On the 22nd of November the regiment received its new colonel, S M Whitside.

The border was calling again, and it was "Back to Texas" on January 29th, 1899 The men were reluctant to leave Huntsville. As a token of the respect they had won there the citizens presented to the regiment a beautiful silk color.

Back in Texas, the troops took station as follows: Headquarters, A, G, H and L at Fort Sam Houston, C, D and M at Fort Clark, B at Fort Ringold, E at Fort McIntosh, F at Eagle Pass, I at Fort Clark, and K at Fort Brown.

General Orders, No 40, War Department, 1898, caused the discharge of 494 "for the duration" men. This in February. When the news—unofficial, at first—arrived that the regiment was to return to Cuba nearly all of these men reenlisted. Sure enough, orders did come, and the Tenth was slated to relieve a volunteer regiment.

Half the troops landed at Manzanillo on May 7, the remainder arrived at Gibara on the 21st. Headquarters A, C and H took station at Manzanillo, L at Bayamo, M at Jiguani, G at Campechuela, B at Gibara, D, E and I at Holguin, F at Banes, and K at Porto Padre. These places will never be forgotten by those who served there. The Cubans were most friendly and obliging, and not a few marriages were celebrated. The sentiment in the regiment was that the stations and service in Cuba were the finest it had ever had.

Field service against insurrectos and bandits was enjoyed for several months, although in the rainy season the difficulties of chasing them down through the jungles were manifold. Lieutenant Walter C Short made one brilliant capture of a band of eleven outlaws after a hard chase. One of these was the famous bandit, Troncon, who won to freedom by acting as executioner for the Province of Santiago. He received credit for five years' imprisonment for every man garroted. It is not known how many men he had to garrote to equal a term of life imprisonment.

Except for a slight epidemic of yellow fever which broke out in H Troop, the troops enjoyed good health.

In January, 1900, the Second Squadron returned to the States—Texas, of course—to function as Depot, or "Home Squadron." Their stay on the Rio Grande lasted just a year, for in April, 1901, they moved to Frisco, thence to Manila, landing on May 13th. A week later they took station in Samar. E Troop, Captain C G Ayres, at Oquendo, F, Captain P E Trippe and 2nd Lieut C A Romeyn, at Calbayog, G, Captain Guy Carleton, at Gandara, H, Captain Robert D. Read and 1st Lieutenant Thos A Roberts, at Mao.

Samar was full of Samaritans, but not any good ones, quoting (now) Lieut Colonel Romeyn. Field service in Samar was very difficult, and to our men, unused to the best method of warfare against insurrectos, had many interesting experiences. Colonel Romeyn writes of one hike: "A few days later E was sent up the Bibotan, G went up the Gandara, H went up on the northwest coast, and F stayed in Calbayog. However, a few days later General Hughes (R P) sent us out, to try us out. We took three days' rations (no cargadores, officers and men carried their own stuff) and a guide and making quite a detour on starting headed for the interior and Luk-Ban.

On the second day we gobbled an outpost and "persuaded" him to lead us to camp. He led us all right. We were soon fired on by another outguard, but he (the prisoner) said the main body was further along.

I had the point and was pushing on when the captain (Trippe) came up and cussed me out for not going after the outpost. I tried to explain, but I went after the outpost and the captain took the guide and went after the main body and found them. They were waiting for him, and had their aim been as good as their intentions F troop would have had some heavy losses, but their bullets flew high and none of our men were hit. We killed two (one being our prisoner, who bolted).

We found and destroyed a lot of bamboo cannon loaded with home-made powder and iron slugs A very good weapon, by the way, at fifty yards, but usually fired at about 500 yards I had a nice climb up a hill about one hundred feet high and came down on my reinforcements. Of course it rained, and that night we had a nice wet camp and marched back the next day to camp.

F troop or detachments made three other hikes but had not other actions except a small one under a sergeant whose name I have forgotten, but a fine man. He was one of the captains of the 48th or 94th, I believe, and he and some scouts marched about thirty miles and had a fight, all in about twenty-four hours And thirty miles in Samar was some hike No roads, and you could not go a mile without using your hands to help you along. One trooper expressed his feelings "Gee, but I wish I was a cavalry horse in these war times"

The Navy one night saw an H troop fire on shore and dropped their second shell on it, the first went high, and by the time the second arrived all 100-yard records had been beaten Roberts made the Navy "set 'em up" for that

E, G and H had a terrible time up in the interior I was Q M at Calbayog and did my best to feed them, but it was a poor bunch of feed I fear

Finally in September (we landed in May) the squadron left for Panay I had received orders for the States and stayed at Calbayog long enough to clear up some of my accountability and then came home

I only remember one good anecdote, but in those days of the "new army" I believe it well worth repeating

One evening Bobby Read was sitting in front of his tent in not the most pleasant frame of mind when a private came up Here is the dialogue as I remember it

Pvt —Sah, I'd like permission to speak to the captain

Bobby—Well, what is it? (rather grouchily)

Pvt —Well, sah, I has a complaint to make agains de fust sergeant

Bobby—(More grouchily)—Well, what is it?

Pvt —Well, sah, de fust sergenat done call me———, and I don like dat sort of thing

Bobby—(More grouchily)—Well, ain t you

Pvt —(Cheerfully)—Yas, sah! yas, sah! If de captain says so

General Chaffee came down to inspect us We received him with a salute of shrapnel fired in the direction of the last reported insurrectos (we got a good echo), and his inspector general (Johnston, I believe) criticised the uniforms After he had gone General Hughes remarked, "Well, if they do their work they can be in their shirt tails for all I care." And we did the work

The squadron remained in Samar until August, when it was moved over to Panay Here the troopers were furnished with remounts, of which many died of Surra Next June (1902) the squadron was slated for a return to the States to join the regiment again It sailed from Manila July 6th and landed at Frisco August 1st, sailing via Nagasaki, Japan Later in the same month E took station at Fort D A Russell, F went to Fort Washakie, G and H garrisoned Fort Mackenzie, all in Wyoming

To return to the troops in Cuba Under the governorship of General Leonard Wood outlawry was abolished and conditions were such that the sub-stations in the interior were reduced in number and the regiment was occupying but two stations, Manzanillo and Holguin In the spring of 1902 several practice marches were taken B and D covered 800 miles, crossing the island twice, A and L covered 525 miles. Pack transportation only was taken

Continuing its policy of moving the Tenth Cavalry around the map, the regiment was ordered back to the States, this time to the northern stations requested by Colonel Mizner long ago. Manzanillo was evacuated April 24th, the troops arriving at Fort Robinson, Nebraska, May 4, via Newport News. The troops at Holguin left that place on May 4, followed the trail and arrived at Robinson May 16th.

Tenth Cavalry colonels continued their popularity with the War Department, for once again the regiment was called on to furnish a brigadier. Colonel Whitside received his star May 29, 1902, and was succeeded by Colonel J. A. Augur, who joined in October.

COLONEL S. M. WHITESIDE

COLONEL J. A. AUGUR

Chapter V.

SERVICE AT HOME

FROM May, 1902, to March, 1907, Fort Robinson, Nebraska, remained the headquarters of the regiment, with the 2nd squadron in Wyoming. During this period there was little to record, excepting the expedition in 1906, when the troops were called out to put down the Utes in Montana.

For the first time in its history, our men had the leisure and opportunity to take up athletics. From the start the regiment made good records. In the words of one old non-com: "What it took to win, we had nothing else but."

1903
TARGET PRACTICE

Regimental order in Army..No. 6
Troop K, order in Army...No. 3
Troop I, order in Army..No. 4
Troop M, order in Army..No. 6
Troop K, order in Cavalry...No. 1

Army Cavalry competition—
    Corporal Logan, Troop K, 3rd medal (Silver).
    Captain Cavenaugh, 4th medal (Silver).

Army pistol competition—
    Corporal Reese, Troop M, 9th (Bronze).

Department Cavalry competition—
(Departments of Missouri and Texas).
    Captain Cavenaugh, 1st medal (Gold).
    Corporal Logan, Troop K, 2nd medal (Silver).
    Captain Hay, 5th medal (Bronze).
    Q. M. Sergeant Anderson, 8th medal (Bronze).
    Corporal Williams, Troop A, 10th medal (Bronze).

Department pistol competition—
(Departments of Missouri and Texas).
    Corporal Reese, Troop M, 3rd medal (Silver).
    Corporal Davis, Troop L, 8th medal (Bronze).

ATHLETICS

Winner of Field Day contests (Headquarters, Band, 1st and 3rd Squadrons), Troop I
Winner of baseball championship, (Headquarters, Band, 1st and 3rd Squadrons), Band. Great interest was displayed in athletics during the year and the results of monthly contests, as published in Department General Orders, show that Fort Robinson (Headquarters, Band, 1st and 3rd Squadrons) stood first in the Department

1904

TARGET PRACTICE

Regimental order in Army	14
Troop I, order in Army	3
Troop K, order in Army	14
Troop A, order in Army	37

In the expert rifleman's test ten (10) qualified—four officers and six enlisted men

Army competition, Cavalry—

Regimental Quartermaster Sergeant B A Anderson, distinguished marksman, 1st medal (Gold).

1st Sergeant Robert Johnson, Troop K, 7th medal (Silver)

Captain William H Hay, 8th medal (Silver)

Army pistol competition—

Sergeant Wm H. Hamilton, Troop D, 12th medal (Silver)

Northern Division Cavalry competition—

Captain H La T Cavenaugh, 1st medal (Gold)

Captain William H. Hay, 9th medal (Bronze).

Sergeant Jesse Baker, Troop H, 12th medal (Bronze).

Sergeant Robert Glover, Troop I, 14th medal (Bronze).

Northern Division pistol competition—

Sergeant Wm H Hamilton, Troop D, 10th medal (Bronze)

Cook William Floyd, Troop K, 11th medal (Bronze).

Q. M. Sergeant Otho J. Woodward, Troop C, 13th medal (Bronze)

ATHLETICS

Winner of gymnasium contest, Troop B.

Winner of field day contest, Troop I

Winner of baseball championship, Troop I

Winner of football championship, Troop B

These contests were participated in by the 1st and 3rd squadrons

1905

TARGET PRACTICE

Regimental order in Army	13
Troop K, order in Army	22
Troop I, order in Army	44
Troop A, order in Army	52

In the expert riflemen test, 20 qualified—four officers and 16 enlisted men

Army Cavalry competition—

Captain W H Hay, distinguished marksman, 10th medal (Silver)

Army pistol competition—

2nd Lieut H S Dilworth, 10th medal (Silver)

Northern Division Cavalry competition—
  1st Lieut Bruce Palmer, 2nd medal (Gold)
  Sergeant Jesse Baker, Troop H, 10th medal (Bronze)
  Cook William Floyd, Troop K, 11th medal (Bronze)
  Captain R J Fleming, 12th medal (Bronze)
  Sqdn Sgt Maj E P Frierson, 16th medal (Bronze)
Northern Division pistol competition—
  Sergeant William H Hamilton, Troop D, 1st medal (Gold).
  2nd Lieut H S Dilworth, 6th medal (Silver).

ATHLETICS

Strict attention was paid to athletic training throughout the year in the line of gymnasium and outdoor drills, contests and games

Winner of indoor contests, Troop B

Winner of field day contests, Troop I

Winner of baseball championship—Headquarters, 1st and 3rd Squadrons, 9 teams—Troop K.

Winner of football championship—1st and 3rd Squadrons, 8 teams—Troop K

1906

TARGET PRACTICE

Regimental order in Army	7
Troop I, order in Army	12
Troop L, order in Army	46
Troop K, order in Army	47

In the expert riflemen test, 49 qualified—eight officers and 41 enlisted men

Army rifle competition—
  1st Lieut Bruce Palmer, 5th medal (Gold)

Army pistol competition—
  Sergeant William H Hamilton, Troop D, 6th medal (Silver)

Northern Division rifle competition—
  1st Lieut Bruce Palmer, 1st medal (Gold)
  Sergeant Benjamin Bettis, Troop A, 14th medal (Bronze)
  1st Sergt Isaac Bailey, Troop B, 23rd medal (Bronze).

Northern Division pistol competition—
  Trumpeter Revere N. Still, Troop K, 1st medal (Gold)
  Corporal Manning H. Reese, Troop M, 11th medal (Bronze)
  2nd Lieut H S Dilworth, 12th medal (Bronze)

ATHLETICS

Winner of field day contests (Headquarters, Band, 1st and 3rd Squadron), Troop I

Winner of baseball championship (Headquarters, Band, 1st and 3rd squadron) Troop K

The Tenth Cavalry seems to have been the Father of Army Polo Lieutenants Palmer, Muller, Cook and Graham were responsible for the phenomenal success of the team, and it was their excellence in this sport that made the Army, for the first time, a factor to be considered in tournaments where civilian teams competed. In 1906, Lieutenants Cook and Graham played on the team which won the international championship in England

A short resumé of the polo seasons follow:

1903

At Fort Logan, Colorado, June 23rd.
  Score:
Tenth Cavalry ... 5 goals
14th Cavalry ... 4½ goals

HANDICAPS

At Colorado Springs, Colorado, June 25, 27 and 29
  Score
Colorado Springs ... 9½ goals
Tenth Cavalry ... 8 goals
  (Handicap of three allowed Tenth Cavalry)
  Score:
Tenth Cavalry ... 6 goals
Denver ... 5 goals
  Score:
Glenwood ... 6¼ goals
Tenth Cavalry ... 5¾ goals
  (Handicap of four allowed Tenth Cavalry)

At Glenwood, Colorado, September.
  A series of games, results not obtainable, was played for the Rocky Mountain championship

At Fort Riley, Kansas, October
  A game was played with a team of officers from Fort Riley for the polo championship, Department of the Missouri, and a cup put up by the management of the Department Athletic Contest
  Score
Tenth Cavalry ... 18 goals
Fort Riley ... 1 goal

1904

Polo was practiced by the officers of Headquarters, 1st and 3rd Squadrons, throughout the open season, and great improvement over the previous year's work was shown
The following are the results of match games participated in by the regimental team
1—Rocky Mountain Championship, under the auspices of the Glenwood Polo Club, Glenwood, Colorado, September, 1904
  Preliminary:
Tenth Cavalry ... 12 goals
Colorado Springs, second ... 1¾ goals
  Finals
Tenth Cavalry ... 4 goals
Glenwood ... 12 goals
2—The Scudder Handicap, under the auspices of the Cheyenne Mountain Country Club, at Colorado Springs, September, 1904
  First Game
Tenth Cavalry ... 9 goals
Colorado Springs, second ... 5 goals

Second Game
Tenth Cavalry .... 5 goals
Colorado Springs .... 0 goals
Third Game
Tenth Cavalry .... 3 goals
Glenwood .... 2½ goals

1905

Polo had been encouraged and practiced by a large number of officers of Headquarters, 1st and 3rd Squadrons, throughout the open season with great benefit to their physical condition and their skill in all branches of equitation

The following are the results of the open championship contests participated in by the regimental team during the year

Tenth Cavalry Challenge Cup, under the auspices of the Officers' Club, Fort Robinson, Nebraska, June, 1905:

First Game
Tenth Cavalry .... 9 goals
Colorado .... 4 goals
Second Game
Tenth Cavalry .... 1 goal
Colorado .... 3¾ goals
Third Game
Tenth Cavalry .... 5 goals
Colorado .... 4¼ goals

Rocky Mountain Championship, under the auspices of the Glenwood Polo Club, Glenwood, Colorado, September, 1905

Preliminary
Tenth Cavalry .... 10 goals
Colorado Springs .... 4 goals
Finals
Tenth Cavalry .... 7¾ goals
Glenwood .... 6½ goals

Western Championship, under the auspices of the Cheyenne Mountain Country Club, Colorado Springs, Colorado, September, 1905

Preliminary
Tenth Cavalry .... 8 goals
Denver .... 6 goals
Finals
Tenth Cavalry .... 8 goals
Colorado Springs .... 1¼ goals

Interstate Championship, under the auspices of the Denver Country Club, Denver, Colorado, September, 1905

Preliminary
Tenth Cavalry .... 12 goals
Denver .... 5 goals
Finals
Tenth Cavalry .... 9¼ goals
Colorado Springs .... 7 goals

Black Hills Championship, under the auspices of the Minnekato Club, Hot Springs, South Dakota, October, 1905

Preliminary.
Tenth Cavalry.. .... 17 goals
Sheridan .. .. ¾ goal

Finals.
Tenth Cavalry.... 8 goals
Sheridan..... 3 goals

The foregoing shows a brilliant season for the regiment in polo, five open championships won, with the unquestioned supremacy of the middle west The officers most distinguished in polo were Lieutenants Palmer, Muller, Cook and Graham

1906

Owing to the marked success of the regimental polo team in the preceding year (1905), four notable players of the East and West, Mr Foxhall Keene, of New York, Mr Bulkley Wells and Bryant Turner, of Denver, and Mr Frank Gilpin, of Colorado Springs, invited the Tenth Cavalry to play a series of polo games at Colorado Springs for the best two out of three games Our team consisted of Lieutenants Muller, Cook, Palmer and Graham, with Captain Paxton and Lieut Cartmell as substitutes.

The results of the games were as follows

April 24th, 1906 ·
Tenth Cavalry . .. 4½ goals
Colorado .. .. 3¼ goals

April 27th, 1906
Tenth Cavalry. ... ... 10¾ goals
Colorado .. .. .. 3 goals

The third game being rendered unnecessary by the success of the Tenth Cavalry, and some of the members of the Tenth Cavalry team having been called away, a handicap game was arranged for which was won by Colorado by a score of 8 to 2¾

Preparation for the autumn tournament was impeded by a tour in a Camp of Instruction for two months immediately preceding the games In fact it was not believed that the regiment would be able to participate until just before the games began The regiment was further handicapped by the absence of Lieutenants Palmer and Adair, the latter who had become first substitute In spite of these difficulties the team participated in all the finals and won a number of notable games.

The team consisted of Lieutenants Muller and Cook, Captain Kromer and Lieut Graham, with Captain Paxton as substitute

Following are the results

Rocky Mountain Championship, at Glenwood, Colorado

Finals ·
Colorado Springs 9½ goals
Tenth Cavalry 6 goals

Interstate Championship, at Denver, Colorado

Preliminary
Tenth Cavalry . 6 goals
Denver .. . 1 goal

Finals:
Colorado Springs...12 goals
Tenth Cavalry..5 goals
Western Championship, at Colorado Springs.
 Preliminary:
Tenth Cavalry...8 goals
Colorado Springs..3¼ goals
 Finals:
Sheridan...8¼ goals
Tenth Cavalry...5 goals
United States Army vs. Civilians.
    Civilians ....9 goals
    Army ....6 goals
America vs British Isles. (Lieutenants Cook and Graham on American team).
    America ....6 goals
    British Isles..4 goals
Woodward Handicaps.
 Preliminaries:
    Tenth Cavalry...13 goals
    Colorado Springs...3¼ goals
           (Handicap of five allowed Tenth Cavalry).

Denver won preliminary from Sheridan, which allowed three goals handicap. On account of the enforced absence of many players the finals were postponed to some future date.

A match game was played with the Sixth Cavalry at Fort Robinson, 1906.

The Tenth Cavalry team consisted of Lieutenants Cook, Adair, and Captain Paxton, with Captain Kromer and Lieutenant Cartmell each playing two periods.

Score: Tenth Cavalry, 12; Sixth Cavalry, 1.

Chapter VI.
PHILIPPINE ISLANDS

JANUARY, 1907, found the troops still in Nebraska and Wyoming. Headquarters, Band, A, B, C, D, I, K, L and M were in Fort Robinson, E and F were still at Washakie, G and H at D. A. Russell. Preparations were being made for a move to the Philippine Islands, so in February E and F joined G and H at D. A. Russell.

March 1st, Headquarters, Band, and Troops A, C, D, K and L entrained for San Francisco, where it was joined March 5th by Major Wint's squadron from D. A. Russell. No time was available to "see the sights" of Frisco. The Transport Thomas was waiting at the dock and received our warriors and steamed away, bound for the land of the Caribao and the festive Filipino. This trip was the second voyage for the Second Squadron, whose veterans put on no end of airs at being seasoned travelers. Honolulu and Guam were touched at, while the troops looked forward to another big reunion.

Manila was reached April 2nd, and the Headquarters, Band, Second Squadron and K and L took station next day at Fort William McKinley. Major Grierson took station at Camp Wallace Union, April 6th, with A, C and D.

Of the troops still at Robinson, Troops B and I entrained May 31st and, following the trail, joined their squadrons in July.

Out of luck, Troop M moved to Fort Riley, Kansas, May 19th and remained until the return of the regiment to the States in 1909, constituting the detachment for the Mounted Service School.

In the Islands the Tenth kept up its record in athletics and military sports against keen competition.

PHILIPPINES DIVISION PISTOL COMPETITION
Corporal Revere N. Still, Troop K, 7th medal (Bronze).
Sergeant Vodrey Henry, Troop H, 10th medal (Bronze).

DEPARTMENT MEET EVENTS
The regiment won the following events at the Annual Athletic Meet of the Department of Luzon which was held in Manila from December 9th to December 14th, competing against

two cavalry regiments, three infantry regiments, one artillery regiment, one company of engineers, and the hospital corps

GENERAL EVENTS

1 —Running high jump
   Private Johnson, Troop B 1st place   Height 5 feet 6 inches
   Private Miller, Troop I, 3rd place
2 —Putting 12-lb shot
   Sergeant Washington, Troop G, 2nd place. Distance 36 feet.
3 —Baseball throwing contest
   Private Thompson, Troop B, 1st place. Distance 321 feet 6 inches
4 —Running broad jump
   Private Davis, Troop F, 1st place   Distance 19 feet 2½ inches
5 —Relay race
   Regimental team, 3rd place
6 —Pole vaulting
   Sergeant Michie, Troop H, 3rd place   Height 9 feet 4 inches
7 —100-yard dash
   Private Loud, Troop I 1st place   Time 10 1/5 seconds
8 —120-yard hurdles
   Private Collins, Troop L 1st place   Time 18 seconds
9—Tug of War
   Regimental team, 3rd place

CAVALRY EVENTS

1 —Mounted wrestling
   Regimental team, 1st place
2 —Tent pegging contest
   Regimental team, 1st place
3—Training of the Squad
   Regimental team, 2nd place

BASEBALL

When the regiment arrived in the islands, April 2nd, 1907, Fort William McKinley was represented in the Manila Baseball League by a post team   1st Sergeant Thompson of G troop was signed by the post team as a pitcher, and proved to be of great assistance in winning for the post the Manila Baseball League pennant for the season 1906-1907

No games between regimental teams of the post were played until the rainy season

As a part of the department meet in December a competition between regimental teams took place. In this competition the Tenth Cavalry team was tied for second place with four other teams, being beaten by three teams of Fort William McKinley which they had beaten several times before the meet

In November a post league was formed consisting of one team from each of the five garrisons at Fort William McKinley   At the end of December the Tenth Cavalry team was leading the league, having won all the games played up to that time

1908

January 7th and 17th to April 8th, Troops E and F, respectively, were stationed in the Mariquina River Valley, and September 11th to October 11th, Troop G, October 11th to November 11th, Troop H, November 11th to 28th Troop K, was stationed at San Mateo,

Rizal, P. I., being engaged in patrolling the Mariquina River Valley, guarding the Manila water supply from infection of cholera.

MARCHES

January 21-26, Troop D, Captain John Ryan, commanding, marched from Camp Wallace Union, P. I., to Camp John Hay and Trinidad, Benguet, and return. Distance marched 187½ miles.

February 10-16, Troop B, 1st Lieutenant William W. Edwards, commanding, marched from Camp Wallace Union, P. I., to Camp John Hay and Trinidad, Benguet, and return. Distance marched 115 miles.

February 23-26, Troops H, I, K and L, under command of Major Robert D. Read, marched through Rizal and Cavite provinces and return. Distance of march 60 miles.

April 18th to May 13th, the Band, under command of 2nd Lieutenant Henry R. Adair, went to Camp Wallace Union, P. I, and Camp John Hay, P. I., and return. Distance traveled about 449 miles.

April 24th to June 11th, Troop I, Captain Henry C. Whitehead, commanding, marched to Camp Wallace Union, P. I., via Camp John Hay, P. I., and return. Arrived at Camp Wallace Union May 13th, where it remained until May 25th. Distance marched 484 miles.

December 30-31, Troop A, 1st Lieutenant Carl H. Muller, commanding, was en route to and stationed at Camp Pasay, near Manila, P. I., representing the regiment at the Philippines Division Annual Military Tournament. Distance traveled 175 miles.

PHILIPPINE DIVISION PISTOL COMPETITION

1st Sergeant Isaac Bailey, Troop B, 23rd medal (Bronze)
Squadron Sergt Major E. P. Frierson, 31st medal (Bronze)

PHILIPPINE DIVISION RIFLE COMPETITION

Corporal William E. Andrews, Troop A, 9th medal (Bronze).

PHILIPPINES DIVISION MEET EVENTS

The regiment won the following events at the Annual Military Meet, Philippines Division, held at Pasay, near Manila, January 13-18:

Steeple chase (2 miles)
  Winner, Captain Robert R. Wallach Time 4.21 1/5.
Officers' flat race (1 mile)
  1st—2nd Lieutenant Emmett Addis
  2nd—2id Lieutenant James S. Greene
  3rd—2nd Lieutenant Henry R. Adair
    Time 1 55 2/5
Soldiers' flat race (1 mile)
  1st—Private J. J. Prather, Troop H
  3rd—Sergeant Ether Beattie, Troop C
    Time 1 55 2/5

MILITARY EVENTS (Cavalry)

Fencing, mounted
Sergeant Richard E. Robinson Troop K, 2nd
Bending race
  1st Corporal Richard P. Parham, Troop K
  2nd - Trumpeter William Trent, Troop K

Time 31 seconds.
Reaching contest.
1st—Private Felix Page, Troop K.
2nd—Corporal William A. McDowell, Troop K.
Time 1 minute 2 seconds.
Individual scouting.
2nd—Sergent William L. Davis and Corporal Alf Williams, Troop K.

Troop K, Captain Harry La T. Cavanaugh, commanding, represented the regiment with great credit at this meet, standing second with 940.69 points.

DEPARTMENT MEET EVENTS

The regiment won the following events at the Annual Athletic Meet of the Department of Luzon, which was held in Manila from December 8th to December 24th, competing against two cavalry regiments, three infantry regiments and one artillery regiment.

FIELD AND TRACK EVENTS

1.—100-yard dash.
   1st place, Private E. T. Loud, Troop I. Time 10 1/5 seconds.
2.—Running high jump.
   1st place, Private G. W. Johnson, Troop B. Height 5 feet 5 inches.
   3rd place, Corporal George Lee, Troop G.
3.—Running broad jump.
   1st place, Private Lee Edwards, Troop E. Distance 20 feet 3 inches.
4.—Putting 16-lb. shot.
   1st place, Private Leslie White, Troop H. Distance 37 feet 3 inches.
5.—120-yard hurdles.
   3rd place, Corporal D. S. Collins, Troop L.
6.—800-yard relay race.
   1st place, Regimental Team. Time 1:29 1/5.

CAVALRY EVENTS

7.—Broad sword contest.
   1st place, Private G. Coleman, Troop H.
8.—Horse training contest.
   1st place, Regimental Team.
9.—Pistol and saber contest.
   1st place, Sergeant William Rose, Troop B.
10.—Tent pegging contest.
   1st place, Sergeant Arthur Baker, Troop D.
11.—Relay race.
   2nd place, Regimental team.
12.—Exhibition drill.
   2nd place, Troop G, (Captain Wallach).
13.—Machine gun contest (Cavalry).
   (a)—To go into action.
      1st place, Tenth Cavalry, 93%. Time 2.27 1/5.
   (b)—Call to arms.
      1st place, Tenth Cavalry, 90%. Time 3:31 4/5.
   (c)—Retiring from action.
      1st place, Tenth Cavalry. (No record).

(d)—Mounted drill
    2nd place, Tenth Cavalry, 87%

GENERAL EVENTS

1—Tug of war
    3rd place, Regimental Team
2—Sparring contest (Middleweight class)
    Winner, Corporal John Henderson, Troop C.

NOVELTY EVENTS

1—Egg and cigar race
    1st place, Corporal J J Prather, Troop H   Time 1 19 1/5

RECAPITULATION:
    Field and track events
        Tenth Cavalry .. . . 42 points, 1st place
    Cavalry Events
        Tenth Cavalry. . ... 72 points, 3rd place
    Machine Gun Platoon Contest (Cavalry)
        Tenth Cavalry.... ....52 points, 1st place

BASEBALL

In the Fort William McKinley League, consisting of one team from each of the five garrisons, for the season 1907-1908 the regimental team stood second

In the Department of Luzon Baseball Tournament, consisting of seven teams, held at Manila, commencing on the 23rd of November, the regimental team stood second, with a percentage of 666

Leading players—

    Best catcher Q M Sergeant S B Barrows, Troop B.

    Best pitcher, fewest hits   1st Sergt W W Thompson, Troop G   (7 hits, 4 games).

In the Post League at Fort Riley, Kansas, consisting of 15 teams, season 1908, Troop M stood first, having won 27 games out of 29 games played

HORSE SHOW

The regiment won the following events in the First Manila Horse Show, held at Manila in March

POLO CLASS
    Captain R G Paxton's black gelding, "Crook," ridden by 2nd Lieut H R Adair
        Blue ribbon

JUMPING CLASSES
    Over 8 jumps, 4 feet 6 inches high
        Cliquot, Troop G, ridden by Captain R R Wallach   Blue ribbon
        Chico, Troop I, ridden by Blacksmith Marts, Troop I   Red ribbon
    Over 6 jumps, 4 feet 6 inches high
        Cliquot, Troop G, ridden by Private Martin, Troop G   Blue ribbon
        Jim Star, ridden by Private Pleasant, Troop G   Red ribbon
    High jump, horse of any country.
        Chico, Troop I, ridden by Blacksmith Marts, Troop I   Blue ribbon   Height 6 feet 1 inch
        Cliquot, Troop G, ridden by Private Martin, Troop G   Red ribbon

Troopers' high jump
> Phil, Troop G, ridden by Private Pleasant, Troop G   Blue ribbon
> Cliquot, Troop G, ridden by Private Martin, Troop G   Red ribbon

Troopers' jump, over 8 jumps, 4 feet 2 inches high.
> Phil, Troop G, ridden by Private Pleasant, Troop G   Blue ribbon
> Chico, Troop I, ridden by Blacksmith Marts, Troop I   Red ribbon

Teams of two horses, over 6 jumps, 4 feet 2 inches high
> Cliquot and Phil, Troop G, ridden by Captain Wallach and Private Pleasant, Troop G   Blue ribbon.

Best trained cavalry horse.
> Guapo, Troop F, ridden by Corporal Alexander, Troop F   Red ribbon

Gentlemen's saddle class—15-1 and over.
> Lieut Emmett Addis, "The Montanan," ridden by Lieut Addis   Blue ribbon

Breeding class, stallions—14 to 15-1
> Captain Whitehead's chestnut stallion, "Padre," ridden by Captain Whitehead. Blue ribbon

Breeding class, mares—14 to 15-1.
> Captain Whitehead's bay mare, "Louise,' ridden by Captain Whitehead   Blue ribbon

Gentlemen's saddle class—14 to 15
> Captain Whitehead's chestnut stallion, "Padre," ridden by Captain Whitehead Blueribbon

Ladies' saddle class—14 to 15-1
> Captain Whitehead's chestnut stallion, "Padre," ridden by Miss Louise Dunn   Blue ribbon

Tandem class
> Captain Whitehead's "Foxy" and "Padre," driven by Lieut Mayo   Blue ribbon

The regiment did not take any part in the competitions in 1909.

The regiment won the following events at the Annual Military Meet, Philippine Division, held at Pasay, near Manila, January 4-16

SPECIAL EVENTS

Enlisted men's flat race—1 mile
> Winner, Sergeant Richard M Norris, Troop A.   Time 2 minutes 3 1/5 seconds

Boxing (Sixth bout)
> Private Frank Wagner, Troop A   Four-round draw

ATHLETIC EVENTS

100-yard dash
> 3rd, Private Deward T Loud, Troop I

Running high jump.
> Winner, Private Guy W. Johnson, Troop B   Height 5 feet 4 inches

Putting 16-lb shot
> Winner, Private Leslie White, Troop H.   Distance 38 feet 8½ inches

120-yard hurdles
> 3rd, Corporal Daniel S Collins, Troop L

Relay race
> Winner, Team from Department of Luzon. (Tenth Cavalry had one man on team)

INDIVIDUAL ORGANIZATION EVENTS (CAVALRY)

Tent pegging.
 2nd, Saddler James N Hines, Troop A
Rescue race.
 2nd, Sergeant Lucius Lemare, Troop A.
Relay race (Mounted)
 Winners, Squad, Troop A.

POLO TOURNAMENT

 Winners, Tenth Cavalry
 Team—1st Lieut Bruce Palmer (Field captain).
  Captain Robert G Paxton
  2nd Lieut Seth W Cook
  2nd Lieut E F. Graham.
  2nd Lieut Henry R Adair
Cavalry Troops
 3rd, Troop A, Tenth Cavalry, 749%
Machine gun platoon
 2nd, Machine Gun Platoon, Tenth Cavalry, 491 66%

The following events were won by members of the regiment at Albany, New York, during the Hudson-Fulton celebration, October 4-9, 1909
Steeplechase (Two miles).
 Winner, Captain R. R Wallach, Tenth Cavalry
Mounted wrestling
 Winners, Corporal Moss, Troop G, and Private Lee Edwards, Troop E
Rescue race.
 Winners, Corporals Williams and Prather, Troop H
 Second, Corporals Moss and Griffin, Troop G
Relay race
 Winners, Sergeant Sibert, Corporal Malone and Privates Little and Coleman, Troop F
 Second, Sergeant Mickie, Corporal Prather and Privates Harrison and Upton, Troop H.
Tent pegging
 Winner, Private Coleman, Troop H
Jumping to form
 Winner, Private Little, Troop F
High jump
 Winner, Private Little, Troop F.
Flat race (One mile)
 Winner, Corporal Malone, Troop F.
Hippodrome
 Winner, Corporal Berrien, Troop E
 Second, Private Sanders, Troop E
Individual horsemanship
 Winner, Private Coleman, Troop H
Shelter tent pitching
 Winner, Troop H

MACHINE GUN PLATOON EVENTS

Machine gun platoon drill and exhibition.
Winner, Machine Gun Platoon, Tenth Cavalry.
Best and most sanitary camp during the week.
Winner, Machine Gun Platoon, Tenth Cavalry.

BASEBALL

In the Fort William McKinley, Rizal, P. I., League, consisting of one team from each of the five garrisons, for the season 1908-1909, the regimental team stood first.

POLO

The following are the results of an inter-regimental polo tournament which constituted a part of the division meet for the Philippines Division Cup, presented by the Army and Navy Club of Manila. The lineup of teams was from the First, Sixth, Ninth and Tenth Regiments of Cavalry.

SUMMARY:

First event, Tuesday, January 5, 1919, Tenth Cavalry vs. Ninth Cavalry.
Tenth Cavalry—Goals earned, 12; lost by penalties, 0; total score, 12.
Ninth Cavalry—Goals earned, 2; lost by penalties, 1; total score, 1.

Fourth event, Thursday, January 7, 1909, Tenth Cavalry vs. Sixth Cavalry.
Tenth Cavalry—Goals earned, 8; lost by penalties, $\frac{1}{4}$; total score, $7\frac{3}{4}$.
Sixth Cavalry—Goals earned, 3; lost by penalties, 0 ;total score, 3.

Sixth event, Saturday, January 9, 1909, Tenth Cavalry vs. First Cavalry.
Tenth Cavalry—Goals earned, 9; lost by penalties, $\frac{1}{2}$; total score, $8\frac{1}{2}$.
First Cavalry—Goals earned, 3; lost by penalties, $\frac{1}{4}$; total score, $2\frac{3}{4}$.

Recapitulation:

Tenth Cavalry—Won 3, lost 0. Percent 100.
First Cavalry—Won 1, lost 2. Percent 33.
Ninth Cavalry—Won 0, lost 3. Percent 00.

The following are the results of two match games played by our Army against a team of English Army officers from Hong Kong, and constituted a part of the Philippines carnival.

First event. Played at Manila, P. I., Wednesday, February 3, 1909.
Second Manila team vs. Hong Kong team.

Hong Kong—
Commander Campbell, Royal Navy, No. 1.
Lieutenant Crookenden, Buffs, No. 2.
Major Findley, Buffs, No. 3.
Lieutenant Green, Buffs, back.

Second Manila—
Lieutenant Adair, Tenth Cavalry, No. 1.
Lieutenant Koch, Sixth Cavalry, No. 2.
Captain Babcock, First Cavalry, No. 3.
Lieutenant Wainwright, First Cavalry, back.

SUMMARY:

Second Manila—Goals earned, 6; lost by penalties, 0; total score, 6.
Hong Kong—Goals earned, 1; lost by penalties, 0; total score, 1.

Second event. Played at Manila, P. I., Sunday, February 7, 1909.
First team vs. Hong Kong team.

Hong Kong—
   Commander Campbell, Royal Navy, No 1
   Lieutenant Crookenden, Buffs, No 2
   Captain Brierly, Royal Artillery, No 3
   Lieutenant Green, Buffs, back.
First Manila—
   W Cameron Forbes, No 1
   Lieutenant Cook, Tenth Cavalry, No 2
   Lieutenant Palmer, Tenth Cavalry, No 3
   Lieutenant Graham, Tenth Cavalry, back

SUMMARY:

First Manila—Goals earned, 9, lost by penalties, 0, total score 9

Hong Kong—Goals earned, 0, lost by penalties, 0, total score, 0

On leaving Manila for the United States, May 15, 1909, it became necessary to dispose of all polo ponies. Among those disposed of, Black Crook (Captain Paxton), had won the first prize, polo pony leass, in the Manila Horse Show both in 1908 and 1909 On arriving at Cairo, Egypt, the Seventh Dragoon Guards offered to furnish mounts and challenged the Tenth Cavalry team to a match game The game was played at the Gizeh grounds June 24th, a team being selected from those officers who happened to be in Cairo

Lineup and results—
   Lieutenant Watson, Seventh Dragoon Guards, No 1.
   Lieutenant Schreiber, Twentieth Hussars, No 2
   Captain Holland, Seventh Dragoon Guards, No 3
   Major Clay, Seventh Dragoon Guards, back
      British goals, 7
   Lieutenant Castleman, No 1.
   Lieutenant Adair, No 2
   Lieutenant Muller, No. 3
   Lieutenant Graham, back
      Tenth Cavalry goals, 1

On arriving at Gibraltar the team hired a sufficient number of ponies and accepted a challenge from the British garrison Although the ponies secured were extremely poor, being employed rather as hunting hacks than as polo ponies, the Tenth Cavalry team managed to make the game fairly interesting

Lineup and results—
   Lieutenant Horner, Norfolks, No 1
   Lieutenant Russell, Gunners, No 2
   Captain Crookson, Bedfords, No 3
   Lieutenant Matthews, Gunners, back
      British goals, 5
   LieutenantMuller, No 1
   Lieutenant Cook, No 2
   Lieutenant Palmer, No 3
   Lieutenant Graham, back.
      Tenth Cavalry goals, 1

On the 18th of April, 1909, the regiment was shocked by the sudden death of its beloved commander, Colonel J A Augur It was thought that a tradition had been broken; heretofore every colonel had won promotion to a brigadier generalcy But alas, Colonel Augur's appointment was en ruote to him at the time of his untimely demise, and the cablegrams congratulating him on his star were impossible of delivery Lieutenant Colonel G H G Gale succeeded to command and remained as such until September 23, 1909, on which date he was relieved by Colonel Thaddeus W Jones.

On May 14th, First Squadron, Major Charles H Grierson, commanding, and on May 15th, Headquarters, Band, and Troops E, F, G, H, I, K and L, Lieutenant Colonel G H G Gale, commanding, left their respective stations, pursuant to General Orders No. 213, War Department, 1908, and General Orders, No 14, Philippines Division, 1909, for Marivels, P. I., en route to the United States

First Squadron arrived at Marivels aboard the U S A. T. Liscum and disembarked about 1 00 p. m May 15th

Headquarters, Band, and Troops E, F, G, H I K and L arrived at Manila, P I. and embarked on the U S A T Kilpatrick about 1 00 p. m May 15th, disembarking at Marivels, P I, about 4.00 p m, same date

About 1 20 p m May 16th the entire command, Lieutenant Colonel G H G Gale, commanding, embarked on the U S A T. Kilpatrick en route to New York City via the Suez Canal, for station at Fort Ethan Allen, Vermont. Arrived at Singapore, Straits Settlements, May 21st. Left Singapore May 24th and arrived at Colombo, Ceylon, May 31st Left Colombo June 3rd and arrived at Aden, Arabia, June 15th Left Aden June 16th and arrived at Suez, Egypt, June 22nd Left Suez, Egypt, and proceeded through the Suez Canal same date, and arrived at Port Said, Egypt, June 23rd Left Port Said June 25th and arrived at Alexandria, Egypt, June 26th Left Alexandria same date and arrived at Valletta, Malta, June 30th Left Malta July 2nd and arrived at Gibraltar July 6th Left Gibraltar July 10th and arrived in New York harbor about 2 00 a m. July 25th. Total distance traveled, 10,729 miles

The regiment remained at New York until July 27th, participating in a civil street parade on July 26th.

Left New York July 27th and arrived at station, Fort Ethan Allen, Vermont, about 2 00 a m July 28th Distance traveled, about 309 miles

Pursuant to paragraph II, General Orders, No 137, War Department, 1909, and General Orders, No 54, Department of Missouri, 1909, Troop M, 2nd Lieutenant Joseph F Taulbee, Second Cavalry, commanding, left Fort Riley, Kansas, July 15th, en route to its station, Fort Ethan Allen, Vermont Arrived at Fort Ethan Allen, Vermont Arrived at Fort Ethan Allen July 18th Total distance traveled, 1,465 miles

August 7th to September 6th, Machine Gun Platoon and Troops A, B, C, D, F and K, Major Charles H Grierson, commanding were participating in the Massachusetts maneuvers Total distance traveled, 381 miles

September 20th to October, Machine Gun Platoon, and Troops E, F, G and H, Major George H Sands, commanding, were en route to and from, and in camp at Camp R S Oliver, New York, participating in the Hudson-Fulton celebration. Total distance traveled, 30 miles.

FORT HUACHUCA, 1920

Chapter VII.

ETHAN ALLEN AND HUACHUCA

THE first winter in Ethan Allen was a long, hard grind, with guard tours walked in blizzards, full pack inspection in weather that caused much comment from our men, who had just come from the neighborhood of of the Equator.

Spring, 1910, brought practice marches into vogue, and the men soon came to know the beautiful country around the post. In July the entire regiment, less D Troop, marched to Pine Camp, N. Y., and until August 30 participated in maneuvers, returning by rail August 31.

Several athletic meets were held, and advantage was taken of the splendid riding hall, a luxury which the regiment had not enjoyed before. The Machine Gun Platoon won the meet held therein in February, 1910; the riding hall events were won by Troop L, while in the gymnasium events Troop A carried off the honors. Field day meets were held during the months of June and September, both being won by Troop I.

Indoor polo was taken up, and in July a team met the West Point team at that place, losing 4 to 1. The West Point team comprised Captains Henry and Long, Twelfth Cavalry; Lieutenants Allen and De Armond, Field Artillery; Lieutenant Zell, Seventh Cavalry, and Lieutenant Cooper, Twelfth Cavalry. Our team was composed of Lieutenants Graham, Adair, O'Donnell, Colley and Van Deusen.

For the first time, the regiment sent representatives to race meets for the army events. The results follow:

At Pimlico, Maryland, May 28th, Army Service Race, one mile flat.

Captain Paxton's mare, "Martha Jane," ridden by Lieut. O'Donnell. Third place.

At Saratoga Springs, N. Y., August 13th, Army Service Race, one mile flat.

Captain Paxton's mare, "Colored Lady," ridden by Lieut. Graham. Third place.

At Pimlico, Maryland, September 1st, Army Service Race, one and one-half miles flat.

Lieut. Scott's mare, "May Lee," ridden by Lieut. Whiting. Third place.

At Pimlico, Maryland, September 3rd, Army Steeplechase, about two miles.

Lieut. Whiting's horse, "Granstark," ridden by Lieut. Whiting. Second place.

At Belmont Park, Long Island, November 8th, Army Service Race, one and one-half miles flat.

Lieut. Scott's mare, "May Lee," ridden by Lieut. Adair. Second place.

BASEBALL

In the Post League, consisting of one team from each organization, Troop A stood first.

The regimental baseball team played a number of games with outside teams both at the post and in towns in the State, winning the majority of the games played.

Nineteen-eleven saw the "usual garrison duties," with the usual practice marches. In September the Inspector General of the Eastern Division, Lieut. Colonel Slocum, took the regiment out for a six-day maneuver around Shelbourne Farms, Vermont. General Bliss camped five days with the regiment at this time.

POST ATHLETIC EVENTS

Indoor Meet—February.

Winner in the meet, Machine Gun Platoon.

Field Day—June.

Winner in the meet, Troop I.

Field Day—October.

Winner in the meet, Troop H.

The following events were won by members of the regiment at Rutland, Vermont, or Governor's Day, September 6th:

Best single horse work. Prize, cup.

Won by Private Weisiger, Troop H.

Best two-horse work. (Team). Prize, cup.

Won by Privates Strawder, Troop L, and Hoge, Troop I.

Best three-horse work. (Team). Prize, cup.

Won by Trumpeter Berry and Private Franklin, Troop A.

Roman Race. (Two horses). Prize, cup.

Won by Private Marts, Troop I.

RACES

The following races were run by horses belonging to officers of the regiment:

At Pimlico, Maryland, May 30th, Officers' Flat Race, one mile:

Lieut. Scott's mare, "May Lee," ridden by Lieut. Adair, first place.

Major Paxton's mare, "Colored Lady," ridden by Lieut. Greene, third place.

At Brookline, Mass., June 17th, Lexington Plate:

Major Paxton's mare, "Colored Lady," ridden by Lieut. Greene, third place.

At Marlboro, Maryland, November 4th, Southern Maryland State Fair, flat race, 1 1/16 miles.

COLONEL THADDEUS W. JONES

Lieut. Scott's mare, "May Lee," ridden by Lieut. Hartwell, second place.

Lieut. Henry R. Adair, riding Troop A's horse, "Anco," won first prize in the International Military jumping event at the Montreal Horse Show in May.

Rutland Horse Show, September 3rd and 4th, high jump won by "Bertie," Troop F.

Jumping competition won by "Bertie," Troop F.

Charger class won by "Jack," Troop F.

All ridden by Lieutenant Hartwell.

BASEBALL

In the Post League, consisting of one team from each organization, the Machine Gun Platoon stood first.

The Regimental Baseball Team played a number of games with outside teams both at the post and in towns in the State, winning the majority of the games played.

BASKET BALL

In the Post League for 1910-1911, ending February 20th, the Machine Gun Platoon stood first, having won all the games it played.

A Post Basket Ball League, consisting of one team from each organization, was organized in November. At the end of the year Troop A stood first, having won all the games it played.

On February 28, 1912, Colonel Thaddeus W. Jones was retired after more than forty years' service. Colonel John C. Gresham was assigned April 3rd but did not join until October 9th.

The regiment had two pretentious marches in 1912 in the Connecticut maneuver "campaign," camping near Berkshire, Conn. This march covered 550 miles.

Major W. A. Holbrook took the Third Squadron and Band to participate in the Rutland Agricultural Fair September 3-5.

In October the First Squadron and Band helped dedicate the Saratoga battle monument at Schuylerville, N. Y.

Continued interest was maintained in sports, as shown by the following:

Indoor Meet—February.

Winner in meet, Machine Gun Platoon.

Athletic Meet—May.

Winner in the meet, Troop A.

RACES

The following races were run by horses belonging to officers of the regiment:

At Bennings, D. C., May, 1912, Remount Steeple Chase, Lieutenant Whiting's "Fico," ridden by Lieut. Whiting, finished unplaced.

At Bennings, D. C., May, 1912, Captain Wallach's horse, "Steptoe," ridden by Captain Wallach, and Lieutenant Whiting riding Troop C's horse, "Colorado," finished unplaced in the fourteen-mile service test.

At the National Horse Show, Madison Square Garden, November 20, 1912, Lieutenant Whiting's "Fico," ridden by Lieutenant Adair, won first place in the broad water jump.

BASEBALL

In the Post League, consisting of one team from each organization, Troop A stood first.

BASKETBALL

In the Post League for 1911-1912, ending March 18, 1912, Troop A stood first, having won all the games it played.

A Post Basketball League, consisting one one team from each organization, was organized in November. At the end of the year Troops A and E and Machine Gun Platoon were tied for first place.

In June, 1913, the regiment left for Winchester, Va., under command of Colonel J. C. Gresham. It arrived July 19th after a march of 720 miles, and camped until September 29 at the Cavalry Camp of Instruction. The Cavalry Brigade did much drilling, marching and peace-time campaigning. On September 30 a move was made to Fort Myer, Va., where the Cavalry Brigade drilled some more and worked out the Tentative Drill Regulations. On the 7th of October the regiment drilled at Potomac Park for two hours and a half for the edification of the War Department. Again on October 9 the Brigade "Stunted" for the President, the Secretary of War, the Chief of Staff and members of Congress.

On October 11 the regiment entrained at Roslyn, Va., and next day was back again at Ethan Allen.

The regiment lived in peace and quiet until November, when rumors grew to a certainty, and the orders arrived placing the Tenth back in the Arizona sector, to practically the same old water holes guarded so zealously way back in the 80's

Troop L, under Captain O P Hazzard, was the first to leave, it departed November 27 and arrived at Fort Apache December 6, 1913 Fort Ethan Allen was evacuated by the regiment on December 5, en route for Fort Huachuca, via the Transport Kilpatrick at Weehawken Galveston, Lewis Springs, Buena and Overton Huachuca was reached on December 19th, and the regiment found itself a permanent home or at least a home station

The Mexican border was in a more than usual turmoil, so five troops were sent out at once for stations. Troop E went to Naco, G, H and M to Nogales, K to Forrest A detachment from A troop was put at Yuma

Colonel Daniel H Boughton was attached to the regiment, and joined July 22, 1914 He commanded from August 1st to 11th Unfortunately he died August 24, 1914

Colonel W. C Brown was assigned September 2nd and joined six days later.

The border stations were not at all attractive The poor little shacks and 'dobes were eagerly sought for by officers and their wives Naco was about as it is now, only more so The usual border patrols were made along the line, enforcing neutrality, and keeping down gun-running Every troop, during 1914, had a tour at Naco; Nogales was garrisoned by Troops A, E, G, H, M and the Machine Gun Platoon at different times during 1914 C troop was at Yuma April 23rd to September 6th, K and D took care of Forrest and Osborne

The siege of Naco, between the Constitutionalistas and Carrancistas, under General Benjamin Hill and General Maytorena, was being fought out in October, and our Head quarters moved there October 7th

An aerial observer would have had difficulty picking out which side was defending At times it looked like a three-cornered fight was due Our men were in trenches and rifle pits all along the line, with machine guns all set for action The Mexicans fought with their customary "sang froid," and enjoyed themselves potshooting across the line The Ninth Cavalry was stationed also in camp at Naco, and they as well as we, suffered casualties from the promiscuous shooting of the warring factions Luckily for us, we had but eight men wounded The Ninth had some killed and wounded The following of "ours" were

    Private Howard Wilson, Troop G, October 4th, shot through body, serious Recovered

    Private Leroy Bradford, Troop B, October 6th, shot through body, serious. Discharged on surgeon's certificate of disability as result of wound

    Sergeant Nathan Stich, Machine Gun Troop, (Troop M), October 17th, flesh wound, hip, slight Recovered

    Cook George J Henson, Troop D, November 18th, back of knee, flesh wound, slight Recovered

    Cassious Clay, private, Troop B, November 27th, right wrist, flesh wound, slight Recovered

    Private John W Miller, Troop H, December 4th, flesh wound four inches below groin Moderate severe Discharged on surgeon's certificate of disability as result of wound

    Sergeant Charles Smart, Troop H, December 6th, left toes, slight. Recovered

    Private Walter Patterson, Machine Gun Troop (Troop A), December 7th, flesh wound left leg, slight Recovered

During this siege a number of horses and mules pertaining to the regiment were shot from stray bullets and killed.

The town of Naco suffered more or less from the artillery fire of the besiegers, several houses being pierced by shells, and buildings near the "line" still bear the marks of many stray bullets. Great difficulty was had in holding back the crowds of visitors from Bisbee and Douglas who flocked to see the "battles," in automobiles, wagons and horseback.

The provocation to retaliate on the Mexicans for the losses sustained while on duty which forbade them to return the fire, was at times almost overpowering. Our men could draw small comfort from the delightful apologies submitted to our commanding officers for the killing and wounding of their comrades, always accompanied by promises that no more shooting would occur. Finally the "siege" drew to a close, and the troops were given a rest and a chance to see what Huachuca looked like. Some of the men, after ten months' service on the border, had not yet seen their home station.

The President was moved to compliment the regiment on its conduct at Naco, in a letter to the regimental commander.

"War Department, Washington, April 7, 1915.

"The Commanding Officer,
  "Tenth U. S. Cavalry,
    "Fort Huachuca, Arizona.
"Dear Sir:
  "By direction of the President, I take great pleasure in expressing to the officers and enlisted men of the Tenth Cavalry his appreciation of their splendid conduct and efficient service in the enforcement of the United States neutrality laws at Naco, Arizona, during November, December and January, last.
    "Very respectfully,
      (Signed) "LINDLEY M. GARRISON,
        "Secretary of War."

Nineteen-fifteen saw a repetition of the work of 1914. The troops rotated on their tours at Naco, Nogales and Lochiel. There were sub-stations at Harrison's Ranch, in the Patagonia Range, and at Arivaca, Sasabe, La Osa, San Fernando soon became well known to our patrols. There was always a chance for a skirmish with the bandits and rebels from across the line, which was quite satisfactory.

On November 21st two privates of Troop F, on observation post near Monument 117, were fired on by Mexicans, and Private Willie Norman was wounded. On November 22nd five armed Mexicans rode into camp at Santa Cruz River and fired upon a detachment of of Troop F, who replied with pistol fire. Mexican casualties believed to be two. On November 25th Mexicans crossed the line and attacked an outpost of Troop F at hill opposite Mascarena's Ranch; one Mexican wounded and made prisoner. On November 25th part of Troop F occupied the western outskirts of the town of Nogales, Arizona, during the seige of Nogales, Sonora, by Carranza forces and were fired on by Carranzistas from Arizpe Hill, Nogales, Sonora, to which fire the troops replied, killing two and wounding others of the Carranza forces.

Troop H was under fire of contending Mexican forces during siege of Nogales, Sonora, November 26th. No casualties.

Troop K, at Lochiel, Arizona, encountered a band of Mexican soldiers who had come across the boundary on August 22nd, rounded up some cattle near the line and was attempting to herd them across to the Mexican side of the line. This was prevented by the prompt action of patrols, who exchanged about 100 shots with Mexican forces. No casualties.

Troops B, E, G and M, under command of Colonel Brown, were at Douglas, Arizona, November 3rd and 4th, during the siege of Agua Prieta, Mexico.

Troops A, B, D, E, M and G, under command of Colonel Brown, rejoined post from Naco on November 24th, and proceeded on November 25th to Nogales, Arizona, arriving there just after the siege of Nogales, Sonora, on November 25th, although Colonel Brown, having preceeded the command, arrived when the engagement was half finished, assumed and retained command until the arrival of Brigadier General Geo. Bell the following morning.

The regiment, except Troops K and L, was inspected by the brigade commander, Colonel Dodd, December 29th and 30th, who reported: "This command seems to be in excellent working condition * * * * officers are very active and much alive to the interest and efficiency of the regiment."

Sergeant Ernest S. Washington, Troop G, graduated at the head of the Non-Commissioned Officers' Class at the Mounted Service School and was highly commended by the commandant of the school.

During the summer months systematic instruction to enlisted men in swimming was given, and an average of about forty-three men per troop taught to swim for short distances.

During August a team of selected men and horses from the Cavalry Division was assembled at Fort Huachuca and trained under the supervision of Captain Babcock, Tenth Cavalry. It took part in the Horse Show at the Panama-Pacific Exposition, and won 57 of the prizes awarded, and $1,165.00 in cash prizes.

During September and October instruction in fire control and approved methods of advancing to the attack was held under Lieut. Colonel Cabell. The results of the final problem, having been submitted for the criticism of the School of Musketry, brought forth a very handsome compliment to the effect that "this regiment is to be congratulated upon attaining the state of training which permitted it to attain such excellent results."

During August, September and October, Regimental Sergeant Major Frierson established a School for Clerks with Regimental and Squadron N. C. O. staff officers as issistant instructors, namely: Reg. Q. M. Sgt. Hugh C. Scott, Reg. Com. Sgt. William W. Thompson, Sqdn. Sgt. Maj. James F. Booker, Sqdn. Sgt. Maj. William F. Scott.

The Department Inspector in his report of the Annual Inspection of the regiment reported: "The Tenth Cavalry is in excellent condition as regards to training and equipment." He also commended Captain Hazzard, commanding at Fort Apache, for "zeal and efficiency in keeping up the post with a depleted garrison."

Chapter VIII.

THE PUNITIVE EXPEDITION

TEXT books and manuals treating of cavalry operations frequently allude to "living on the country" and acting as independent cavalry, but it is rare that our cavalry has actually but put to such a test. This, however, did occur with the Tenth Cavalry in the Punitive Expedition from March 20th to April 20th, 1916. It was, with the exception of two days' rations carried in the saddle bags, practically without one mouthful of government rations, a grain or spear of government forage, or a cent of government money, and there had been no picking of men or horses for the trip.

On March 8, 1916, the country was startled by the raiding of Columbus, New Mexico, by a strong party of Villistas, led by the famous Pancho himself. Numbers of buildings were wrecked or burned, and in spite of gallant resistance of the Thirteenth Cavalry, which was surprised, severe casualties occurred among the civilian population and the troopers. The Villistas were driven off and pursued by several troops of the Thirteenth. Scores of dead and wounded Villistas in and around Columbus and on their trail southward testified to the ferocity of the engagement.

About 11:30 a. m. March 9th, the regimental commander, Colonel W. C. Brown, and Adjutant Captain S. McP. Rutherford were going over routine work in the old amusement room that served as an office, when the telephone rang and the hard working adjutant picked up the receiver with a bored expression which soon changed to one of intense interest as he called back: "Call up Douglas and see if you can get any further details"; then turning to the commanding officer he said: "Colonel, the telegraph operator phones that an Associated Press dispatch has just gone over the wires saying that Villa attacked Columbus early this morning, burned half the town, and killed a lot of civilians and solders." It was now the commanding officer's turn to wake up, and he ordered 'Get that word around to troop commanders at once and tell them to hold their troops in readiness for orders,' adding, "We'll get them soon enough." These came about thirty minutes later from Cavalry Brigade Headquarters at Douglas, directing that the command proceed to Douglas at once equipped for field service.

The wheels were thus set to turning in earnest. The entire command, less Troops L, M and the Band, started at 4 p m, equipped for the field with equipment "A" and two wagons per troop, and with the regimental pack train, for which last they were in the next four months to thank the guardian angel of the Tenth Cavalry. The regiment was escorted to the limits of the post by the band and by a following of the non-combatants who were left behind. Little did they know at this time that the regiment would not return for a year, and some of its members—never!

The War Department and Congress were for once in complete accord regarding an expedition to follow the bandits into Mexico, and bring back "Villa, dead or alive." General Pershing was named Commanding General of the Punitive Expedition, to the delight of the Tenth. Little time was lost organizing the columns for their chase into Chihuahua.

Culberson's Ranch, New Mexico, was designated as the rendezvous for the Second Cavalry Brigade, to consist of the Seventh Cavalry, Tenth Cavalry, and Battery B of the Sixth Field Artillery. That night the regiment made the first camp at Hereford, twenty-five miles out. Culberson's ranch was reached on March 13th, via Douglas, Forrest, Slaughter's Ranch and Hood's Ranch, picking up Troops D and G en route.

The 14th and 15th was spent in getting rid of most of the equipment brought along. Everybody was to travel "very light." With Villa's trail a week old, and getting colder every hour, there were wiseacres who predicted that the expedition would never even get in touch with his band, much less catch him in his chosen haunts among the mountains of Chihuahua. Much remained to be seen. It was the Cavalry's 'day out.'

Even at Douglas men did not know what was the ultimate destination, which was safeguarded with more than customary success. The brigade commander could not state positively whether it was intended to cross the line, although he felt very sure that it would be done.

Naturally each troop quartermaster sergeant had loaded his troop wagons with more plunder than Noah would have carried, and equally naturally they almost wept when they saw it remorselessly thrown over and stored at Douglas. The space on the wagons thus made was filled with extra ammunition of which the regiment had all too little for a long campaign. At this place Captain C B Babcock was taken seriously ill with appendicitis and was left behind to undergo an operation.

Lieut Colonel D R Cabell was also detached here under orders to report as Chief of Staff to General Pershing.

On March 15th the following orders issued in quick succession

HEADQUARTERS SECOND CAVALRY BRIGADE
Culberson's, N M March 15, 1916

Field Orders,
No 1

1 This command will be prepared to move at once on the receipt of orders

2 Pack transportation only will be used. Five days' rations will be carried. All ammunition and forage for which transportation is available will be carried

3 The guard to be left in this camp will consist of dismounted men only. All transportation and stores left in this camp will on the departure of the command, be assembled

in the vicinity of the present Brigade Headquarters. An officer to command the dismounted guard will be designated by the commanding officer, Tenth Cavalry.

By order of Colonel Dodd:

E. W. EVANS,
Major, Tenth Cavalry, Adjutant.

Copies furnished:
Co. Tenth Cavalry.
Co. Seventh Cavalry.
Co. Baty. B, 6th F. A.

HEADQUARTERS SECOND CAVALRY BRIGADE.

Slaughter's Ranch, New Mexico, March 15, 1916.

Field Orders,
No. 2.

Advance Guard.
Troops A and B,
7th Cav.

Lt. Col. Tompkins,
Commanding.
Main Body.

Colonel Dodd,
Commanding.

7th Cav. less 3 troops;
10th Cav. less 4 troops.
Batty B, 6th F. A.

Battery Guard.
1 Tp. 10th Cav.

Rear Guard.
1 Tp. 10th Cav.

1. The location of the enemy is unknown.
2. Some of our troops have crossed the line into Mexico in the vicinity of Columbus, New Mexico. This command will proceed at 12:30 a. m. March 16th in an endeavor to meet the enemy.
3. (a) The advance guard will leave their camp at 12:30 a. m. March 16th.
   (b) The main body will follow the advance guard at a distance of five hundred yards.
4. The outpost will be relieved as the command passes, joining the organization to which they pertain.
5. The pack trains will follow immediately in rear of the command.
6. The hospital ambulances with sanitary wagons will follow in rear of the regiments to which attached.
7. The commanding officer, Tenth Cavalry, will supply a rear guard of one troop, which will march in rear of the pack trains at a distance of 50 yards.
8. The commanding officer will be found at the head of the main body.

By order of Colonel Dodd:

E. W. EVANS,
Major, Tenth Cavalry, Adjutant.

Copies furnished:
Comdg. Genl. P. E. U. S. A.
Regimental Comdrs.
Commander of Artillery.

At 1:15 a. m. March 16th, the command crossed the line south of Culberson's Ranch, and was fully committed to the task. There was no moon and the night was bitterly cold; the road was choked with clouds of white alkali dust that obscured everything so that the pack train got lost in the darkness and did not rejoin the column until it had camped at Carriza Springs about 6 a. m., where a little water was found. Page one of the War Diary shows that the command halted at 6 a. m., to water, groom and feed, resuming the march at noon. Three day's rations was carried on saddle. By 6:30 p. m., Ojitas was reached, fifty-eight miles from Culberson's.

In view of the experiences of the next four months it will perhaps be interesting to know that at Culberson's Ranch the wagons were ordered to proceed to Columbus, and that before leaving the wagons, all the curb bits were removed and packed and left with the wagons, as were also the overcoats and other bulky articles of clothing and equipment, and on the subsequent hard marches it was often wished that the sabers had likewise been dropped. There were no cooking utensils except five nested sheet iron buckets that by a fortunate mistake on the part of someone were packed on the pack train.

Colonia Dublan was reached the next day after a hard march of fifty-two miles over rough trails. Several horses fell behind, but the stragglers all arrived by late in the night. The 18th was spent in camp near Colonia Dublan on El Rio Casas Grandes. This camp was made in the dark in a great field of dry grass that was nearly four feet high and so dry that the troop commanders did not dare to allow a fire. The men were so tired and sleepy that no one dared take a chance of a grass fire that would certainly stampede the horses. Accordingly camp was made on the bank of a stream. The rest of the three days' grain carried on saddles was consumed this date. The three days' ration of bacon carried on the pack train was turned over to the Seventh Cavalry who were moving south that night, and from this date until April 20th no government chow was forthcoming. (Efforts were made later to allow the organizations to get ration credits for their abstinence; without avail. Naturally.)

On the 19th, the unfit men and horses of the First and Second Squadrons were left at Colonia Dublan with Troops I and K. The squadrons proper entrained for points south on the M. N. W. R. R. (See Appendix "F.") The train for the two squadrons arrived about 10 a. m., and from the assortment of rolling stock available it was found that twenty-five box and cattle cars and three flat cars were either barely serviceable or could be made so. This would transport the First and Second Squadrons, Machine Gun Troop and Pack Train only, leaving I and M troops behind. One locomotive only was on hand.

Previous occupants of many of the cars had deliberately built fires on the floors so that holes two feet or more in diameter had burned through and had to be patched over. Box cars had to have ventilators cut in the ends before the animals could be loaded. Doors in some cases being missing had to be replaced by nailing boards across the open spaces.

The conductor and engineer spoke no English, and talk with them was only through the interpreter. To effect repairs, camp hatchets, a few axes and a couple of saws only were available.

By 5 p. m., however, the squadrons were loaded, and left at 5:30 p. m., with the animals in the cattle and box cars, impedimenta and as many men as could stick on them on the flat cars, while the remainder rode on the car roofs where they were barricaded from a possible fall by bales of hay along the edge of the roofs. They traveled in truly Mexican style.

While loading, it was discovered that there was no fuel for the wood-burning engine, so a part of the corral—for which the government later paid $1,900.00—was loaded on the tender. The conductor intended to stop at Casas Grandes for more fuel and water, but reflecting that the natives there were probably hostile, concluded to go on to Don Luis where everybody turned out and loaded fuel from another corral. Five times in ten hours the engine ran out of either water or fuel and troops had to detrain and "rustle" for telegraph poles, mesquite, old ties, parts of corrals and anything else that would burn. One man would have been left in his search for fuel but he was a good sprinter and easily caught up with the train.

At Kilometer No. 282, No. 41 American airplane was found wrecked, and from data thereon it was discovered that the pilot had been R. H. Willis, Jr. The engine having stalled here, the train was parted and the First Squadron sent two miles further south to

Rucio, the engine returning for the remainder of the train. In seventeen hours after leaving Colonia Dublan the train, by most strenuous efforts, had made twenty-seven miles.

Colonel Brown took the Second Squadron and the Machine Gun Troop, detrained at El Rucio and camped in the mountains twenty-four miles away, en route to San Miguel. Major Evans with the First Squadron continued the rail trip southward. The "foraging" brought beef and corn. San Miguel was reached, but the expected meeting with Villa was postponed. It was the usual type of Mexican ranch; a huge central building of stone and adobe. All the rooms opened on a central patio, doors occasionally loop-holed for rifle fire, and a high breast wall so placed that the establishment could be defended if necessary. A few yards from the central building a stone wall surrounded the corral so that it, too, could be defended from the house.

Not only were no signs of Villa discovered, but he evidently had not been near here, though the man in charge of the ranch reported that Villa had been in the vicinity of El Valle on the Sunday proceding.

On the 23rd, at El Toro, the First Squadron joined Headquarters. Their's had not only been a fruitless chase, but their train had been wrecked, injuring about sixteen men of Troops A and B. The next camp was at La Osa, via Namiquipa. A Mexican cavalry regiment joined the column at Namiquipa to cooperate, but these turned back after a short stay. They had a hunch.

Lieutenant Nicholson, Seventh Cavalry, came into camp carrying dispatches, and unfortunately had taken from their bearers and brought back to the commanding officer Tenth Cavalry, two dispatches which had been sent out by the latter. Weather warm in day time, but ice a quarter inch thick on streams at night.

Viewed in the light of subsequent events it is probably a fact that too much confidence was placed in the so-called Carrancista forces cooperating with the expedition. Villa, bandit though he was, had many qualities which made him a hero in the eyes of the Mexican peon. The rapid advance into Mexico and sudden appearance at their very doors with troops, mounted, armed and equipped in a manner which few of these people had ever seen, probably dumfounded them and created in their simple minds a feeling that against this Colossus of the North they must make common cause, and, while ostensibly friendly, were actually shielding Villa.

On the 27th information was received that Villistas occupied Sta. Catarina Ranch a few miles eastward of La Osa. Starting at 3:30 a. m. on the 28th, a fine surprise attack was delivered, but as no resistance was offered, something was wrong. Villistas the inhabitants undoubtedly were, but proof was lacking. Information was given, however, that he surely was to be found at Rubio. At Quemada, en route, it was learned that Villa and a large command had passed through there but three days previous. Several Thirteenth Cavalry horses captured at Columbus were picked up here, having been ridden nearly to death by the fleeing bandits.

The inhabitants of Quemada were manifestly unfriendly; available provisions and forage were hidden away upon the approach of our troops and the announcement made that there was none to be had anywhere. San Diego del Monte was the next camp. A severe snow storm on the 31st caused great suffering. On April 1st the First Squadron was left behind at San Diego del Monte, the other troops marching to Aguas Calientes. Here the first engagement was had.

The advance guard surprised the Villistas, 150 strong, under a chief named Beltran.

A dismounted fight ensued resulting in their retreat to a wooded ridge in the rear of the settlement. Under cover of the overhead fire of the Machine Gun Troop, Troops F and H assaulted the ridge, and drove the band off in confusion. A running fight of seven miles ensued, when night fell. The horses were in such poor shape that there was no chance to overtake the bandits, who were provided with fresh mounts. Three Villistas were killed and several captured. They abandoned a machine gun pack outfit in their flight. Although the trail was picked up early next morning, and followed for two days, it soon became impossible to follow, the bandits scattering in ones and two in many different directions. (See Appendix "G.") San Antonio was reached on the 3rd of April. The question of lack of funds had now become serious. The securing of supplies by means of receipts was clearly not a workable arrangement, and sooner or later was likely to bring on open hostilities with the civilian population. A Cusi citizen described the receipt method as follows:

"You Americans pay for food all right, but you give receipts only. Now you buy a cow from a man who lives a hundred miles from any railroad. Even if that railroad were operating, it would be six months before he gets his mail. You take that cow and you kill it and give him a receipt. He mails that receipt to the quartermaster at San Antonio in Texas. It takes, maybe, six months for it to get there, if it gets there at all. When the quartermaster gets it, he cannot pay for it. He returns duplicate vouchers to be signed. They take another six months to reach the man, and then he cannot write and cannot read English. If he can do all of these and signs in the proper place—even then he gets, about eighteen months later, a check that he cannot cash."

Here the regiment learned that the Seventh Cavalry had had a big fight with Villistas at Guerrero on the 29th day of March. Villa, severely wounded in the leg, had left the place the night before the attack. He had been shot by some natives impressed into his service.

On the 6th orders arrived via airplane directing a move on Parral, with a view to cutting off Villa's retreat through that place. It was said that Villa was carried on a stretcher and by carriage. (See Appendix "B.") The march was taken up through Cusihuirachic, where much needed supplies were secured from the mining company there. Carranza soldiers were attached as scouts and guides. La Joya was reached via Cieneguita on the 7th. An informer brought the news that Pablo Lopez, a lieutenant of Villa's, was hidden in the town. Arrangements were made to seize him, but at the last minute the informer disappeared, and in the darkness it was not possible to locate the hiding place. The inhabitants were most unfriendly. No local guides could be induced to serve.

While in Satevo the commanding officer and guide, the former with a quantity of Mexican silver, hunted up the principal inhabitant of the little village asking for corn and fodder, at the same time displaying the silver with some ostentation, saying, "Nosotros pagamos por todos." (We pay for everything). The place, it seems, had been raided in turn by contending Mexican factions (Carrancistas taking even women's clothing) until there was but little left, and that little was kept well hidden.

When they learned that the accursed "Gringos" were actually paying for supplies, their astonishment knew no bounds; one native telling the interpreter, "Why, it's like seeing Christ come down from heaven, to see you paying for what you want!" We were taken across the creek to a little adobe hut, and on the door being unlocked a sight met their eyes which caused them for the moment to forget all their troubles—two rooms filled with corn fodder! It is needless to say that for once the hungry, tired horses got a good feed.

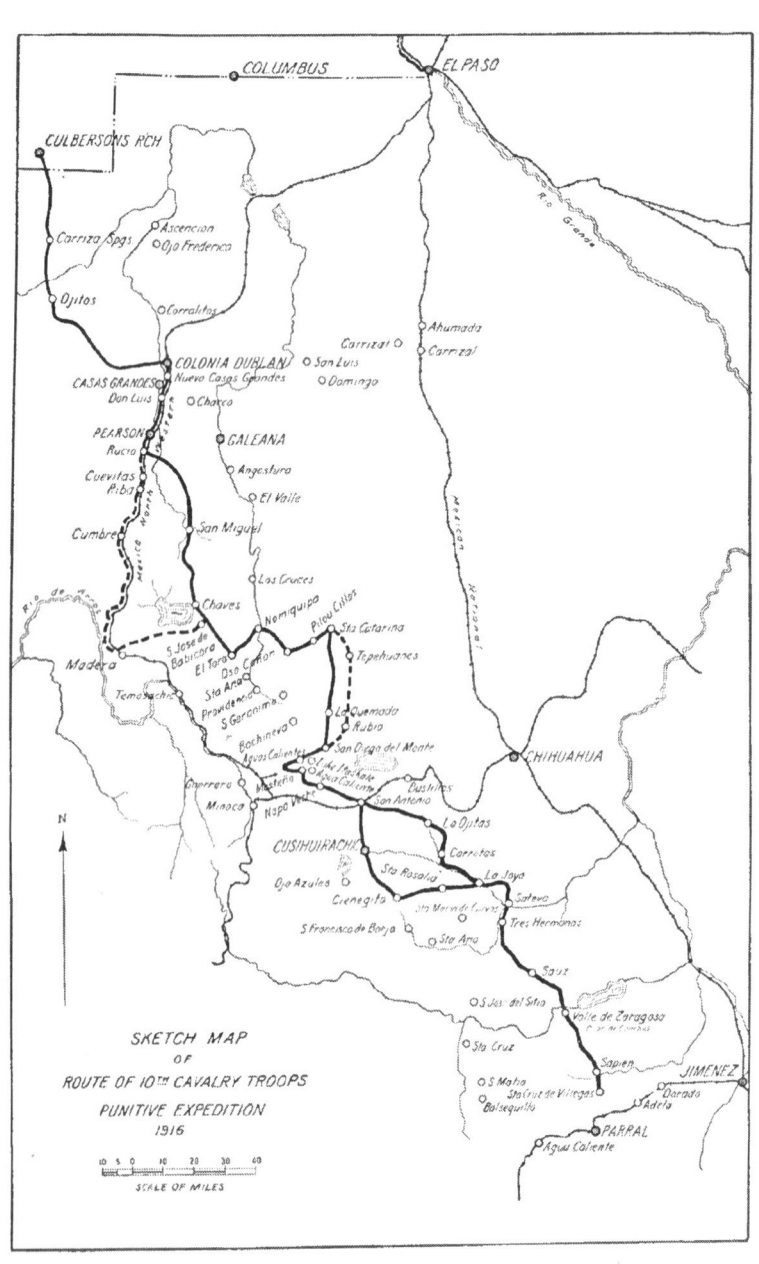

CAPTAIN CHARLES T. BOYD
KILLED AT CARRIZAL, MEXICO, JUNE 21, 1916

The news of their paying for the things spread, and in the course of a couple of hours they had more eggs and chickens offered for sale than they could buy.

The natives crowded into camp intent on seeing and examining everything carried and worn by the Soldado Americano; in fact they got so chummy that some one borrowed Lieut. Adair's field glasses and forgot to return them.

On this march, as at other times, the road passed through and by whole square miles of fields formerly under cultivation, and although this was the planting season, no preparations were being made, save in the gardens about the houses, for raising a season's crop. The reason was apparent; the better the crop the surer it was to be levied on by one or the other of the contending factions. So what was the use!

On the 11th, marched eighteen miles to Valle de Zaragoza where camp was made in a grove (the town park) in the edge of town on the banks of a fine stream. Twenty Villistas were in town yesterday and were raiding a cloth factory when Major Tompkins' arrival compelled them to drop their loot and run. This part of the regiment had now lost twenty-eight animals. Natives here were unusually curious and friendly and, dressed in their best, crowded into camp. Captain Mesa, a Carranza officer, was very helpful in securing supplies.

Sapien was reached on the 12th, via Tres Hermanos, El Suaz and Valle de Zaragoza. While in camp at Sapien word was brought by three Thirteenth Cavalry troopers that their squadron (two troops) had had an engagement with the Parral garrison and was retreating. They had been cut off in the pursuit.

Camp was immediately broken, and the command moved at once to the support of Major Tompkins' squadron, which was found in a defensive position at the Santa Cruz de Villegas. Upon the arrival of Colonel Brown's force (the Second Squadron and Machine Gun Troop) the Carrancistas withdrew from their menacing position. (See Appendix "I.") The situation remained very tense. Parral was about ten miles distant to the south. Those in the expedition did not realize the storm of protest and indignation that swept the country when the news was brought that Carrancistas had made such an unprovoked attack. It had been assumed that cooperation, not antagonism, was to be met in the pursuit of the bandit who was menacing the Carranza government. Read General Pershing's letter to Colonel Brown. (Appendix "J.")

Supplies were very short, and foraging for same was very discouraging. On the 15th, Lieutenant Troxel and a detachment of twenty men were held up while on a hunt for a camp site on the railway and informed that they were prisoners; that they must accompany the Carrancistas to a camp southeast of Parral. Lieutenant Troxel couldn't see this at all, and returned to his camp at Santa Cruz without incident. Reinforcements under Lieut. Colonel Allen and Major Howze arrived on the 15th, but the promised supplies from Parral were held up. In the face of this, a proposal was received from General Lozano to move Mexican troops through Santa Cruz to reinforce the Parral garrison. The bodies of the dead troopers of the Thirteenth Cavalry were buried in the village cemetery with honors.

Colonel Brown in a report to General Pershing writes:

"The greatest care has been taken to do no injustice to natives of the country. The chief difficulty from the outset has been to do this and still to secure the necessary supplies from a country which has been raided in turn by Villistas and Carrancistas. To maintain my command on this expedition I have already advanced the government over $1,453.00 of

FIRST LIEUT. HENRY R. ADAIR
KILLED AT CARRIZAL, MEXICO, JUNE 21, 1916

CAMP AT COLONIA DUBLAN

personal funds. Other officers have advanced several hundred dollars. How or when we will ever be reimbursed is problematical.

"One thing, in my opinion, is certain, and that is that to seize supplies whether the owner is willing or not will sooner or later result in hostilities. Major Tompkins agrees with me most emphatically.

"I hope it will not be taken amiss that I am putting this matter strongly, but I do so with a feeling that it is perhaps not thoroughly understood. The condition of this command at this date is such that if Villa were known to be within say thirty miles we could doubtless march there and defeat him, but to attempt any further marches without additional remounts may be regarded as impracticable.

"When we left Casas Grandes March 19th everything pointed to our ability to capture Villa in about five (5) days, and the orders were such that we took no forage for the squadron and have but one saddler's kit for the command. From the commanding officer down, all baggage has been carried on our horses. I am so short even as to paper that it has been no little embarrassment, and I am writing this letter on paper given me by a native, and writing it fine to economize in material.

"Upon questioning yesterday the presidente of Parral as to Villa's whereabouts I got but little satisfaction. He was thought to be in the Guerrero district they said—one report at Sta. Ana and another at Concepsion. They either do not know, or if they do they give evasive replies. People who have recently been looted of horses and goods show the most discouraging apathy in trying to rid the country of this bandit."

On April 18th two wagonloads of supplies arrived from Parral, including a lot of civilian trousers. These were much needed, for many of the men were by this time in rags. Dr. McMurdo graphically described the situation in a wire which he sent to Fort Huachuca, viz: "Send me a pair of trousers. Am getting sunburned." Captains Rutherford and Pritchard with Troop C arrived on the 20th with a train of 36 pack mules, $2,300.00 (coin) for purchase of supplies, and the mail. (The first received since entering Mexico).

After a period of watchful waiting, at the end of which it was ordered that no further move would be made southward, the command left Santa Cruz for station at the Satevo base. There were now present: 34 officers, 606 enlisted men, 702 horses, 149 mules, requiring six tons of hay and over 9000 pounds of grain a day. To supply a command of that size required a base on a railroad, and the regiment was now some 350 miles, as the crow flies, from Culberson's Ranch—over one-third the distance from there to the City of Mexico.

M troop joined here on the 25th. Later orders directed a move to San Antonio, which was reached by easy stages on May 1st. The command remained here until the 5th, resting and recuperating, then moved on to Lake Itascate. Headquarters, M and Machine Gun Troop went on to Namiquipa, Major Charles Young commanding, in the absence of Colonel Brown, sick. Namiquipa was reached on the 8th. The First Squadron and Troops I and K joined here. On the 12th the Second Squadron rejoined Headquarters at Namiquipa. Civilized tobacco was available for the first time.

On the 15th, Namiquipa was evacuated except for Troop E, left as escort for the artillery, and the march for Colonia Dublan taken up via the river road, said road crossing the river seventy-one times between Namiquipa and El Valle. Troop L joined here on the 17th. Camp was made at Colonia Dublan two days later. A camp site was assigned and the place was no sooner occupied than it was changed in a terrible wind storm to a new site. After two more moves it was found that the new site was the worst that they had yet been in, so they were permanently assigned to it and the men set to work to build adobe walls on which to pitch their shelter tents. Considerable ingenuity was shown in making cots of poles and other devices for camp comfort. While at this place the wagons arrived, but every bed roll and field desk had been looted by every one through

1. Col. Evans; 2. Gen. Dodd; 3. Capt. Kromer; 4. Col. Dade; 5. Capt. Kennington; 6. Maj. Lindsey; 7. Dr. Porter; 8. Capt. Smith; 9. Lt. King; 10. Capt. Rodney; 11. Dr. Barber; 12. Capt. Trozel; 13. Maj Cavenaugh; 14. Capt. Lohn; 15. Lt. Hoge; 16. Capt. McCornack; 17. Dr. Demmer; 18. Lt. Migdalski; 19. Lt. Abbey; 20. Maj. Pritchard.

whose hands they had passed, so that nothing remained except those things that had long since been discarded as useless.

Now began the long, tedius routine of camp life in Mexico, with but outpost duty and scouting to relieve the monotony. The Eleventh Cavalry was camped alongside the Tenth. Remounts were secured from Columbus in June.

In the middle of June the Third Squadron took outpost stations at Corralitas Ranch, Ojo Federico and Vado de Fusiles.

Reports of activities of the Mexicans became more and more disturbing. Word was given out that the Carranza government had announced that no opposition would be made to Amercian troops retiring to the northward, but that any troops venturing to move in any other direction would be opposed. Several brushes with native troops had occurred as a result of these orders and affairs were becoming daily more strained when the Carrizal incident occurred. On June 22nd, four men of Troop C arrived in camp bearing the news that Troops C and K had clashed with Carrancistas at Carrizal the day previous, and that Captain Boyd and Lieutenant Adair were among the casualties. Later in the day men from K troop straggled in, confirming the news.

When reports of the opposition of the Mexicans to the movements of American troops in any direction except toward the north became current, two troops of the Tenth were ordered out from Colonia Dublan on a scout. Troop B, under command of Captain Gardenhire, was directed to move out to Ojitas, the ranch where we made our second camp in March on the way into Mexico, to ascertain whether there were any troops in that vicinity. Troop C at the same time was ordered to go through a town called Carrizal to Ahumada. Troop C, Captain Charles T. Boyd commanding, with First Lieut. Henry Rodney Adair and thirty-nine enlisted men, left camp on the morning of June 20th on what was to be the last ride for many of them.

Boyd was a man of unusual force and a natural leader; Adair was one of the finest horsemen in the regiment and had acted as Regimental Adjutant in March and April.

The trail took them over a rough country to the northeast. After they had marched about eighty-five miles they reached the San Domingo ranch which was in charge of an American. Along with them went an American guide, Lon Spillsbury, a reliable man and a first class interpreter. At San Domingo ranch, Troop K, under Captain Lewis Morey, was met with and the troop accompanied Troop C under the command of Captain Boyd. Carrizal lay about eight miles to the east of San Domingo ranch and Villa Ahumada lay about eight miles to the northeast of Carrizal. After camping for the night at the ranch the march of the two troops was resumed. The land toward Carrizal was open grass land varied with a few swales. It was not timbered and there was no cover. The trail lay across an open mesa that was fringed to the front at the edge of the town of Carrizal with a few cottonwoods along a stream bed, and across which a barbed wire fence ran quite close to the town. Approaching the town the column first came to an irrigating ditch that was filled with water. As they drew close to the town it was seen to be occupied, and on a nearer approach being made a party of Mexican officers rode out to meet the approaching troops. The Mexican commander told Captain Boyd that he could not allow passage through the town of American troops. To him Captain Boyd replied that his orders required him to go through the town and that he must do it. A long discussion ensued, the Mexicans opposing the entry of the troops, the American commander insisting on his orders. It is reported that finally the Mexican commander offered to allow the two troops to pass through the town in column of fours, but fearing a trap this was declined. At any rate the discussion closed by the Mexican returning to the town and the prompt disposition for attack by the two troops whose combined strength was less than eighty men. The led horses were sent to the rear and the troops were formed in line of skirmishers, Troop K being well to the right, with orders to protect the right flank. With this disposition the line moved forward.

As the line drew closer to the edge of the mesa where a barbed-wire fence edged the creek, fire was opened on them from two machine guns that the Mexicans had cleverly disposed under cover. The fire was returned, but the machine gun fire had already played havoc with the horses, stampeding several of them. C troop, charging forward, lost Captain Boyd, who was shot first in the hand, then in the shoulder, and then as he sprang out of the irrigation ditch to lead his men he was shot in the head and instantly killed. Lieutenant Adair took the troop and carried it forward, storming the town. The two machine guns had previously been put out of action by the hot fire from Troop C. At this stage of the fight Troop K, on the right flank, came under a heavy flanking fire from some Mexican soldiers in a cottonwood grove, and a party of Mexican cavalry appearing at that moment on the right flank of Troop K, that troop fell back, leaving the right flank of Troop C exposed to the hostile fire. Lieutenant Adair, having advanced to the line of the houses in the town, found that his men were short of ammunition and went back to get the belts from the wounded, of whom there were quite a few. As he came back he was shot while crossing the irrigation ditch. The bullet struck him just above the heart and he died a few minutes later. The troop having no officers with it, the men became confused and realizing that they were opposed by tremendous odds, and that they had no support, for K troop had retired, they retreated, but not until they had inflicted a loss of about eighty on the enemy, including their commanding general.

The horses of both troops, stampeded by the bullets that went into the herds, did not stop till they came to the San Domingo ranch where the men found them later. The two troops, losing all cohesion, dropped back to the ranch and got the horses. There were no officers for the men, for both of the Troop C officers had been killed and Captain Morey had been wounded.

The losses were as follows: Killed—two officers, seven enlisted men. Wounded—one officer, ten enlisted men.

Twenty-one enlisted men were made prisoners, but were returned June 29 at El Paso, Texas, after many privations.

The results of this skirmish were widespread, and all the forces longed for an opportunity to come to real hand-grips with the Mexicans, but this was not the intention of the authorities. Only the State and War Departments know what amount of diplomatic correspondence ensued. It seemed for a time as if a casus belli had been brought about; perhaps our impending entrance into the World War was the main consideration. It is not the purpose of this history to register surmises on mysteries.

Camp at Colonia Dublan lasted all summer; yea, even to fall. Bets were made that the election had something to do with the duration of camp. The work at the camp at Dublan was again taken up and the rest of the summer and fall was spent in perfecting equipment of the regiment and in training, for by this time it was pretty well realized that the time would soon come when America would enter the World War. The autumn was cold and windy and men were set to work building adobe houses and kitchens. At this work they showed remarkable aptitude and in a few weeks the entire regiment was in comfortable winter quarters. By this time a remarkably satisfactory service with the border had been established and frequent truck trains brought supplies and mail at regular intervals.

While in camp at Dublan the regiment celebrated its fiftieth birthday by a very clever program that was gotten up by Major Charles Young, assisted by the sergeant major and some of the first sergeants.

During the summer months Major Evans was promoted and took command of the regiment, and Captain W. L. Luhn was appointed adjutant.

Christmas was ushered in by a cold norther and the Christmas dinner and its accompanying festivities, which had long been planned, was entirely spoiled by the tremendous wind storm that will be long remembered by every one who was in Mexico at that time. Whole steers that were being barbecued were so covered by the clouds of dust that they were uneatable, and the troops had to seek what shelter they could. Very few men ate at all for twenty-four hours.

The slogan of "Villa, dead or alive," was heard no more in Mexico. In January, word at last came that the troops were to withdraw from Mexico, and the march homeward began on January 30th, 1917. The regiment marched with the rest of the column to Columbus, reaching there on February 5th, and took up the march for its home station at Fort Huachuca, where it arrived on February 14, 1917.

Chapter IX.

1917-1921

BACK in Huachuca, it was but a short time until the declaration of war against Germany. Persistent rumors existed throughout the summer that a cavalry division was to be organized and sent over, but later events indicated that our role was not to be an active one abroad.

The call for officers for the National Army came straight to the veterans of the Tenth Cavalry. A total of sixty-two non-commissioned officers were commissioned—twenty captains, twenty-three first lieutenants, and nineteen second lieutenants. See Appendix "M" for the complete list. In all, the regiment sent 600 of its old men to form a nucleus for organizations, who were appointed First, Mess, and Supply Sergeants.

The National Army drew also from the officers of the regiment. Practically all the older officers were promoted to field rank, and several won their stars. The new officers from the training camps were good material, and the regiment "carried on." Officers gained, 50; lost, 39, during the year.

Eight hundred and fifty recruits joined between April and June. A recruit detachment was organized and the men fully instructed before assignment to troops.

Hope for overseas service was not lost; a trench system was constructed "up the canyon," and all the doughboy stunts were practiced. Gas masks and grenades were startlingly new for self-respecting cavalrymen.

The Headquarters Troop baseball team won the championship trophy cup without losing a single game. In the Liberty Bond Drive this troop also won the cup for the highest subscription with a total of $17,800.00, a per capita of $214.56.

The border patrol kept on the job as usual. The First and Second Squadrons took tours garrisoning Nogales, Lochiel and Arivaca, while the Third Squadron kept one troop at a time at Naco. Troop L remained at Fort Apache, where it had been stationed previous to the Punitive Expedition, and where it returned after coming out of Mexico.

At Nogales were two troops, and one each at Lochiel and Arivaca, when, in August, 1918, German activities, working in the fertile soil of the Mexican mind, began to take aggressive shape in this quarter of the world.

About August 15, 1918, the Intelligence Division reported the presence of strange Mexicans, plentifully supplied with arms, ammunition, food and clothing, gathering in increasing numbers in and about Nogales, Sonora; also the presence of several strange white men, apparently Germans, at times engaged in addressing gatherings of Mexicans, explaining military terms, movements and methods. At about this time an anonymous letter was received, written by a person who claimed to have been a major in Villa's forces, who was sickened and disgusted at the atrocities committed by Villa and his men, and at the lack of pay or reward, and who claimed a feeling of friendly respect for the American troops, warning them of the German influences at work near and in Nogales, advising of the financial activities of the German agents, and of a contemplated attack on Nogales about August 25, 1918. This letter rang so true that it became a subject of investigation by Lieutenant Colonel Frederick J. Herman, Tenth Cavalry, then acting Sub-District Commander at Nogales, and Lieutenant Robert Scott Israel, Infantry Intelligence Officer at Nogales, and so many points of the letter were verified that it was given more than ordinary weight.

Shortly after the receipt of the warning letter, daily and nightly activity on the part of the Mexicans was observed on the hills overlooking the American city of Nogales, Arizona, and commanding the roads traversing the gulch in which the city lies, where trenches were being constructed.

At this time the Thirty-fifth Infantry, under orders for a change of station to Camp Travis and France, was leaving Nogales in detachments of a few companies at a time, and on the morning of August 27, 1918, it was generally believed in Nogales, Sonora, that the infantry had all gone, leaving the garrison of the camps but two troops of the Tenth Cavalry.

About ten days prior to August 27th, Colonel Herman requested reinforcements, including the Machine Gun Troop of the Tenth Cavalry, advising the district commander at Douglas, Arizona, of the situation at Nogales. Two troops were sent, with the injunction to send one to Arivaca.

About 4 p. m. of August 27, 1918, the infantry line guard at the customs gates on International Avenue became involved in a fight with armed Mexicans, either customs guards or Mexican soldiers—probably the latter—and within a few minutes the whole infantry was engaged, every hill-top on the Mexican side showed its intrenchments filled with armed men, and the fight was on.

Lieutenant Colonel Herman, on the way to Nogales from his camp two miles west of the town, stopped a truck roaring toward camp, and learning the facts telephoned his cavalry camp and then instantly drove back to take command of the troops. By the time his car had raced over the two miles the three troops of the Tenth were mounting and at once proceeded to Nogales at a gallop. The squadron consisted of Troop A, Captain Roy V. Moreledge; Troop C, Captain Joseph D. Hungerford, and Troop F, Captain Henry C. Caron. In the meanwhile the three companies of infantry under Captain Marshburn were being assembled and brought to town in motor trucks by the quartermaster.

The Tenth Cavalry was dismounted and the led horses sheltered in the side streets. Troop F, Captain Caron, was assigned to Titcomb Hill and the west end of International

Avenue. Colonel Herman took charge of the infantry in the center at the railway depot. Troop A, Captain Moreledge, was sent to Morley Avenue, ready to advance across the line, if necessary. Captain Hungerford, with Troop C, was placed in reserve near Reservoir Hill, and the infantry ordered to move up Reservoir Hill, preparatory to clearing the heights to the south of their position. Some difficulty arose here, and the infantry not moving forward as desired, were withdrawn and held in reserve, and Troop C moved up into place. During this movement, Companies G, F and H, Thirty-fifth Infantry, were coming into positions assigned them, as fast as they arrived from camp, and extend along the American front. Company F on Reservoir Hill, Company G on Titcomb Hill, and Company H as a reserve, with a detachment at the Southern Pacific station. During the distribution of the American troops they fired but little, but the Mexican fire was very heavy. Several civilians in the American city were hit, and a number of soldiers wounded and one killed. It became necessary to return the Mexican fire as a measure of self-defense. The sheriff of Santa Cruz County—Sheriff Earhart—was directed by Lieutenant Colonel Herman to round up and confine all armed citizens in the City Hall, as they were getting in the way and complicating matters.

The Mexican fire now grew heavier, and Lieutenant Colonel Herman decided to clear the line of houses on the Mexican side of International Avenue of the numerous snipers operating from the doors and windows, particularly in and near the Concordia Club, and Captain Moreledge, with Troop A, was directed to clear this terrain and gain a commanding position among the rocks overlooking the Mexican town, which was done promptly and in a most creditable manner. Simultaneously, Captain Hungerford was directed to advance from Reservoir Hill across the line and clear the heights in his front, then holding intrenchments filled with Mexicans. After crossing the line and while moving forward in frontal attack, Captain Hungerford was shot through the heart and instantly killed. Several of his men were wounded at this time, but the advance never faltered, led by the first sergeant, until the crest was gained and the rifle pits and trenches cleared of dead Mexicans.

At 4:45 p. m. Lieutenant Colonel Herman received a gunshot wound in the right leg while directing the advance across International Avenue by a sniper from a building nearby. At about the same time, Captain Caron, moving his men from point to point toward the Mexican side, was shot through the right arm. Both of the wounded officers, after a first aid treatment, resumed their places with their troops. Lieutenant L. W. Loftus, Thirty-fifth Infantry, was also fatally wounded about this time.

U. S. Consul E. M. Lawton and Sheriff Earhart at 5:50 p. m. delivered a message from the Mexican Consulate requesting the U. S. troops to put up a white flag and to cease firing and that the Mexicans would also. Colonel Herman's reply was that if firing from the Mexican side did not cease within ten minutes he would come over the line with the balance of his forces and burn Nogales, Sonora, to the ground.

The American fire from the captured hillsides, and the rocky position of Troop A, and from the buildings in Nogales, Arizona, had become very effective and the Mexicans were losing heavily. Assisted by Lieutenant Israel, of the Intelligence Division, and the Sub-District Adjutant, Lieutenant James B. Potter, Tenth Cavalry, Lieutenant Colonel Herman was pushing the fighting at all points, when at 6:00 p. m. the Mexicans ran up a white flag at the Custom House, without ceasing their fire, however.

At 6:15 p. m., Colonel Herman, accompanied by U. S. Consul Lawton and Lieutenant Israel and a bugler, proceeded to the U. S. Consulate in Nogales, Sonora, under a constant, heavy fire directed upon this group, although the U. S. Consul displayed a white flag made of his handkerchief. At the Consulate the Mexican representative met the party and arranged for the cessation of fire and the restoration of normal conditions. Once, during the conference, the Mexican commandant demanded the weapons of Colonel Herman and Lieutenant Israel. He was told they might try to take them. A rather tense moment ensued, but the alert position of a detachment of the Tenth Cavalry rifles covering the group in front of the Consulate, some one hundred feet away, prompted the Mexican commandant to think better of the proposition. The American fire ceased at command when the conference began, and after some delay the Mexican fire ceased also.

It was agreed to suspend hostilities until 7 o'clock the following morning, by which time it was hoped matters would adjust themselves, the Mexican officials denying participation of government forces in the battle and insisting that it was the work of independent and irresponsible Mexicans, strangers in the town.

After the conference, American headquarters were established at the National Hotel, to which Colonel Herman repaired after having his wound dressed, and where he remained until 5:30 of the following morning, when relieved by Brigadier General Cabell. During the evening the positions of the troops were strengthened, rations and forage and ammunition distributed, and preparations made to finish the affair in the morning. During the night a trainload of armed Mexicans arrived from Hermosillo, but no disturbances occurred during the night.

The arrival of the Machine Gun Troop and several other troops of the Tenth Cavalry, and some artillery from El Paso on the following day, settled all disturbances for the time being.

In this action the infantry was commanded by Captain R. J. Marshburn. Colonel Herman, during the engagement, received the voluntary offer of the services of Major H. B. Cheadle, infantry, on leave at Nogales, Arizona, and of Captain James T. Duke and Lieutenant Scott, Tenth Cavalry, which were duly accepted.

The forces engaged were the Tenth U. S. Cavalry, Troop A, 86 men; Troop C, 82 men; Troop F, 90 men, with 587 enlisted men and 12 officers of the Thirty-fifth Infantry, and one officer and 30 men of the Q. M. Corps.

The officers of the Tenth Cavalry engaged were:
    Lieutenant Colonel Frederick J. Herman.
    Captain Joseph D. Hungerford.
    Captain H. C. Caron.
    Captain Roy V. Moreledge.
    Captain James T. Duke.
    Lieutenant Wm. Scott.
    Lieutenant James B. Porter.
    Lieutenant S. M. Lockwood.

First Sergeants Thomas F. Jordan, Troop F, and James T. Penny, Troop C, were specially commended by Colonel Herman for their promptness, intelligence and efficiency in assuming command of their respective troops, and carrying on the work when their officers were shot down.

The total losses in the American forces were two officers, three enlisted men and two civilians killed, and two officers and twenty-nine enlisted men wounded. On September 15, 1918, the Intelligence Department had reported a total of 129 Mexicans buried as a result of gunshot wounds received August 27, 1918, also two Germans, presumably officers, who were shot while directing Mexican troops (?)—armed men, acting as troops—and an estimate of 300 Mexicans wounded.

The final estimate of the Mexicans engaged was 2400 men.

The losses of the Tenth Cavalry were:

Killed—Captain Joseph D. Hungerford, Troop C.

Wounded—Lieutenant Colonel Fred J. Herman; Captain H. C. Caron, Troop F; Sergeant Arthur E. Green, Troop A; Private Ulysses S. G. Clayton, Troop C; Private Van Gibson, Troop F; Private J. E. Harris, Troop C; Private Charley T. Johnson, Troop A; Private Wallace Reynolds, Troop A; Private Orvel Walls, Troop A.

During this entire engagement the discipline and conduct of the Tenth Cavalry was excellent, the most careful regard to existing orders and the laws of civilized warfare being exercised, and hostilities ceased when no longer necessary.

The Headquarters Troop team won the 1918 baseball championship cup. The football cup was won by Troop F from the Machine Gun Troop team after an exciting Thanksgiving Day game. Boxing was greatly stimulated by the Y. M. C. A., and McDuncan of the Machine Gun Troop was recognized as the champion in the "manly art." Three desultory games of polo were played with the First Cavalry, all of which the Tenth won. The Regimental Baseball Team in 1919 won eight games out of ten played, but lost a series of three games to the Twenty-fifth Infantry, losing two. In the District Field Meet our team won from the Twenty-fifth Infantry, Nineteenth Infantry, First Cavalry, with a score of 45; Twenty-fifth Infantry, 34; the others combined, 9.

POLO

February, 1920, saw the revival of polo, a large turnout starting practice. A shipment of ponies arrived via Fort Bliss, but after being picked over by the five teams there the remainder were not superior to the best troop mounts. An average of eighteen players turned out for games every Wednesday and Sunday. Major John A. Robenson was designated as polo manager during the summer, and much is due his able and energetic organizing. A separate polo stable was established, with picked men from each troop. As a result the ponies were carefully trained, their exercise supervised, and the equipment kept in top notch condition.

In the elimination tests for the Eighth Corps Area, the Tenth won from the First Cavalry in two games.

Lineup, Tenth Cavalry.	Lineup, First Cavalry.
1. Major J. A. Robenson.	1. Lieutenant Duffy.
2. Captain L. G. Hefferman.	2. Lieutenant Holt.
3. Lieutenant H. S. Stanton.	3. Captain Snider.
4. Captain E. L. N. Glass.	4. Lieutenant Robinett.

Score: First game, 12-1; second game, 9-4.

Play at El Paso was under very adverse conditions. Captain Hefferman had his shin laid open by a kick in play at Douglas, and played with a football shin guard. Major Robenson and Lieutenant Stanton collided in practice, the former suffering a brain concussion and Lieutenant Stanton receiving a blow on the back which required him to play standing in his stirrups. The two ponies, our best, were also laid up. The team had to play the Seventh Cavalry, winners of the Fort Bliss tournament, and was swamped by the scores of 29-1 and 15-2. Some consolation was derived from beating the Eighth Cavalry 6-2 in six periods.

In January and February, 1921, four games were played with the First Cavalry.

Lineup, Tenth Cavalry.
1. Major Robenson.
2. Lieut. Healy, Lieut. Holt.
3. Major Glass.
4. Colonel Winans.

Lineup, First Cavalry.
1. Lieut. Robinett, Major Briscoe.
2. Lieutenant Holt.
3. Lieutenant Colonel Wm. Scott.
4. Colonel F. Le J. Parker.

Score: First game, 8-7 (won); second game, 2-9 (lost); third game, 8-6 (won); fourth game, 10-7 (won).

In April, 1921, the Eighth Cavalry was invited to come up to Fort Huachuca to play, we furnishing the mounts. Each team won a game.

Lineup, Tenth Cavalry.
1. Major Robenson.
2. Major Menoher.
3. Captain Lawrence.
4. Major Glass.

Lineup, Eighth Cavalry.
1. Captain Finley, Goodier.
2. Captain Smith.
3. Captain Upton, Carl.
4. Colonel Langhorne, captain.

Score: First game, 6-2 (won); second game, 8-9 (lost).

In a return tournament at El Paso the Eighth Cavalry mounted our team; the team won from a picked team 10-1, and defeated the Eighth by the score of 6-5. The prospects for a good showing in the coming Corps Area Tournament appear bright.

The "Buffalo Bulletin" was started May 5, 1920, as a small five-paged mimeographed news sheet. Later, the Regimental Press furnished an attractive cover and ran twelve pages. Its circulation expanded from two hundred to twelve hundred, and had a mailing list of over two hundred. It carried the doings of the regiment to its many ex-officers, retired men and friends. The letters received proved that their affection for the old regiment was still lively. The Bulletin ran until May 12, 1921, when it was ordered discontinued, having run foul of the rulings of the Committee on Public Printing, that no paid advertising could be carried in any official or semi-official publication. It was necessary to carry ads to cover the cost of the cuts, photos, and the yellow paper for the cover.

In June, 1920, the Arizona District Athletic Team, composed principally of men from the Tenth Cavalry and the Twenty-fifth Infantry, won the Southern Department meet, a tryout for the Army Olympic entrants. This team scored 160 points, all other teams combined, 45. The Tenth Cavalry was strong in the track events, the Twenty-fifth Infantry predominant in the field events.

Troop F, Captain Duke commanding, left the post June 2, 1921, to garrison Fort Apache. Troop I, our last organization there, was relieved in April, 1919, by a troop of the First Cavalry.

The Eighth Corps Area Rifle and Pistol Competition was held at Camp Bullis, Texas, in July. Our competitors upheld the reputation of the Tenth Horse in fine style.

The Pistol Team won the Championship Trophy Cup from the fourteen competitors, with a score of 7904, sixty-nine points ahead of the runnerup, the Fifteenth Field Artillery.

THE TEAM

Staff Sergeant William T. Wright, Headquarters Troop. (Gold Medal).
Sergeant Marcus Nelson, Troop M. (Gold Medal).
Corporal William R. Thomas, Troop A. (Silver Medal).
Private Allen Peterson, Troop K. (Silver Medal).
Corporal Pryor Sharp, Troop I.

Private Abbey Anderson, Troop L.
Sergeant William Johnson, Troop B.

Major J. V. Knznik ranked thirteen in the pistol competition and won a silver medal.

The Rifle Team finished third among nineteen entries, four points behind second place, and only fourteen points behind the winner, the Twenty-third Infantry Team. The nearest cavalry competitor was the Eighth Cavalry in eighth place. Officers were not eligible to shoot on regimental rifle or pistol teams.

Private William F. Tillman, Troop D, led all competitors in the rapid fire scoring, but due to extremely adverse conditions in shooting at 1000 yards, causing fine shots to turn in scores such as four to six, or even total misses, he scored but a ten and eighteen. An average score by him or a team-mate at 1000 yards would have won the trophy.

Private Tillman finished in eighth place (Gold Medal), Corporal James W. Powell, Troop E, in fifteenth place (Silver Medal), First Sergeant Clifford A. Sandridge, Troop H, in twentieth place (Silver Medal), Corporal John A. Jeter, Troop C, in thirty-fourth place (Bronze Medal), out of 254 competitors.

General Dickman, Corps Area Commander, complimented the regiment in the following letter:

HEADQUARTERS EIGHTH CORPS AREA

Fort Sam Houston, Texas, July 16, 1921.

From: Commanding General.
To: Commanding Officer, Tenth Cavalry, Fort Huachuca, Ariz.
Subject: Commendation.

1. It gives me great pleasure to congratulate you upon the excellent showing made by your regiment in the Corps Area Rifle and Pistol Competition.

2. The fact that the Pistol Team, representing your regiment, won the trophy by outshooting all other pistol teams in this corps area, indicates a high degree of training and morale in your command.

(Signed) J. T. DICKMAN,
Major General, Commanding.

Two polo games were played with the First Cavalry on July 3rd and 17th. The first game at Douglas, Arizona, (on their ponies) was halted after four chukkers because of rain. Score: Four to three in favor of the Tenth Cavalry.

THE TEAMS

Tenth Cavalry.	First Cavalry.
No. 1—Lieutenant Sampson.	No. 1—Lieutenant Jackson.
No. 2—Captain Holt.	No. 2—Captain Duffy.
No. 3—Captain MacNabb.	No. 3—Lieutenant Colonel Scott.
No. 4—Captain Kenahan.	No. 4—Captain Holt.
Lieutenant Healy.	

The same teams lined up on our home field on our ponies July 17th; Major Clifford, fresh from Riley, playing No. 1 for the visitors. The game was fast and exciting, but our team came out on top with the long end of a 9 to 8 score.

Chapter X.
THE MACHINE GUN TROOP

THE machine gun was born of American inventive genius many years before 1906—but it was not until that year that our army commenced to appreciate the weapon by providing a temporary organization of a platoon in each regiment of cavalry and infantry. The platoon consisted of one officer and twenty-one men detailed from the first three troops of the regiment.

The organization was effected in July, 1906, at Fort Robinson, Nebraska, with First Lieutenant Albert E. Phillips detailed to organize and command the unit. Starting with a clean slate and a new mechanical weapon it was a simple matter to arouse enthusiasm among the men.

In March, 1907, the platoon sailed with the regiment for the Philippine Islands, remaining there until 1909, when it returned to the States via the Suez Canal for station at Fort Ethan Allen, Vermont.

THE DEVELOPMENT OF INDIRECT MACHINE GUN FIRE

It is perhaps not generally known that indirect machine gun fire originated and was developed in the Machine Gun Platoon of the Tenth Cavalry. The European war is credited with the development of machine gunnery. Six years before this war, during the 1908 training season in the Philippines, the Machine Gun Platoon demonstrated the feasibility and practicability of direct overhead and indirect machine gun fire. This work of the Tenth Cavalry platoon was discussed in Europe and printed in service journals from England to Australia.

At a meeting of the Aldershot Society held in England, Major General Cosgrove presiding, after an extended discussion of the machine gun development in the Tenth Cavalry, dismissed the meeting with the remark: "Gentlemen, we may all go home, believing as the American does, (referring to First Lieutenant Albert E. Phillips, Tenth Cavalry) that the successful handling of machine guns requires hard study and patient experiment."

From this beginning in 1908, the platoon, and later the troop, continued the development of machine gunnery, having perfected many methods of fire supposed to have originated during the European war.

The overhead employment of machine guns to protect troops—the "barrage" of the war—was actually employed in tactical exercises by the machine guns of the Tenth Cavalry several years before the war.

There are methods of fire to this day known only by a few of the old Tenth Cavalrymen who belonged to the organization during the years 1908 to 1917.

The Machine Gun Troop used overhead fire during the engagement at Aguas Calientes, Mexico, April 1, 1916, to advance a detachment going forward to capture Mexicans firing from an adobe hut.

The 1915 edition of Applin's British Machine Gun Tactics (one year after the beginning of the war) carried an article on Indirect Machine Gun Fire by the Tenth Cavalry.

The original platoon of 1906 was enlarged and reorganized as a provisional troop in 1914, with Captain Albert E. Phillips detailed as its commander.

THE MACHINE GUN TROOP IN THE PERSHING EXPEDITION IN MEXICO—1916-1917

The troop, under command of Captain Phillips, marched six days from Fort Huachuca, Arizona, to Culberson's Ranch, New Mexico, before crossing the border. It crossed at midnight of March 16th, 1916, making the forced march with the regiment of one hundred twenty (120) miles to Colonia Dublan, arriving on the evening of the 18th. The march southward was resumed the evening of the 19th, the troop being attached to the squadron under Colonel Brown. It participated in the action at Aguas Calientes the morning of April 1, 1916.

The assembly of the cavalry on the outskirts of Parral, Mexico, found only the Tenth Cavalry with machine guns; all other machine gun troops having fallen out and being left behind.

Every soldier that left Colonia Dublan with the troop was present at Parral.

The troop marched over eleven hundred (1100) miles before settling down in camp on the return to Colonia Dublan.

The reorganization of cavalry by eliminating machine gun units from the regimental organization disorganized and breaks up a troop whose record for machine gunnery as well as other lines is believed to be second to none in the United States Army. This brief history would not be complete without quoting the remarkable record established from 1906 to 1912:

HEADQUARTERS TENTH CAVALRY.
Fort Ethan Allen, Vermont, December 22, 1912.

General Orders,
No. 23.

Six years ago the Machine Gun Platoon, Tenth Cavalry, was organized at Fort Robinson, Nebraska, with First Lieutenant Albert E. Phillips detailed as its commander. Since that time its record has been an uninterrupted series of victories whenever it entered into competition with other organizations. Some of its records are so remarkable that they cannot fail to stir the pride of every officer and soldier in the regiment.

It was not until 1908 that contests with other organizations began, and this is the result:

In 1908—First place; prize, silver cup; Machine Gun Competition Military Meet, Department Luzon. Winning 52 out of 60 points, with two cavalry and three infantry regiments entered.

In 1909—First place; prize, silver cup; Machine Gun Drill U. S. Military Tournament during the Hudson-Fulton celebration at Albany, N. Y.; two infantry regiments competing. First place; prize, silver and gold shield for "Best and most sanitary camp for entire week," eleven organizations contesting for it.

In 1910—First place, Tenth Cavalry, Indoor Meet, (Gymnasium and Riding Hall); prize, banner.

In 1911—First place, Regimental Indoor Meet; prize, banner. First place, Regimental Baseball League; prize, silver cup. First place, Basketball League; prize, banner.

In 1912—First place, Regimental Indoor Meet; prize, banner.

The world's recognized record for speed in machine gun work is accorded the Machine Gun Platoon, Tenth Cavalry, in: "Machine Gun Tactics, Applin, England."

1st—Platoon in line at halt, moved forward in section column at gallop for 200 yards, went into action and fired in 31 seconds. Military Meet Department Luzon, Manila, P. I., 1908.

2nd—Platoon in shelter tent camp, animals on picket line 15 yards in front. At signal, horses were saddled, mules packed, platoon formed and moved over an irregular course for 500 yards, went into action and fired in 3 minutes and 21 seconds. Military Tournament and Athletic Meet, Department Luzon, Manila, P. I., 1908.

3rd—With guns packed on mules and gun squads dismounted, the guns were unpacked, set up, loaded and fired, barrels exchanged, reloaded and fired the second itme, in 25 1/5 seconds, both guns firing simultaneously. Nearest competitor, 52 seconds. Philippine Division Military Meet, Manila, P. I., 1909.

Lieutenant Phillips, prompted by a keen desire to develop the Machine Gun Platoon as a potent factor in warfare, has contributed a valuable chapter on "Indirect Fire With Machine Guns" to Captain Applin's book, England, bearing the title of "Machine Gun Tactics."

The regimental commander makes of record the splendid achievements of Lieutenant Phillips and commends them to the consideration of his comrades now that his service with the Machine Gun Platoon, by operation of detached service law, is ended.

By order of Colonel Gresham:

G. J. ODEN,
Captain and Adjutant, Tenth Cavalry, Adjutant.

M. G. T. Athletics

In 1915—Baseball champions of the regiment; prize, silver cup.

In 1918—Baseball champions of the regiment; prize, silver cup.

In 1919—Baseball and football chimpions of the regiment; prizes, silver cup for each.

Sergeant S. C. Williamson of this troop won the championship 100 and 220 yard dashes in the Arizona District Meet on July 27, 1919; won the championship cup of the Southern Department in the 100 and 220 yard dashes on June 8, 1920, at Camp Travis, Texas, and won the Championship of the Army in the 100 and 220 yard dashes at the Army Meet held in St. Louis, Mo., July 5, 1920.

Vale

The regiment is now awaiting the reorganization, which requires a consolidation to six troops, and headquarters and service troop. Many non-commissioned officers will lose their warrants, being surplus over the new Tables of Organization. But this is all in the game, and the regiment has lived through many reorganizations in the past.

* * * * * * * * * * *

So ends the written history of the Tenth Cavalry in so far as printed words can briefly and succintly set forth the facts concerning acts which called for courage, endurance and self-sacrifice.

The regiment is proud to have had upon its rolls the names of the officers and men who fought the savage tribes of the Southwest, who participated in the Cuban and Philippine Campaigns, and who went across our southern border in the Punitive Expedition.

The stirring days of the pioneer are gone, the hostile Indian is no more, but the traditions of the regiment, the spirit of cooperation between officer and man, the comradeship of the Tenth and the loyalty to the Buffalo Standard—these still exist.

Knowing these things, we look forward with confidence to the future, and predict that the record of the Tenth Horse will be continued unblemished and untarnished, and that, when the old regiment is again put to test, they will be found true to their motto, "READY AND FORWARD."

Finis

Commanding Officers, Tenth Cavalry

Colonel Benjamin H. Grierson	Organization, 1866; Dec. 1, 1888
Lieut. Colonel Geo. C. Hunt	Dec. 2, 1888; Aug. 20, 1890
Colonel J. K. Mizner	Aug. 21, 1890; Jun. 7, 1897
Lieut. Colonel T. A. Baldwin	Jun. 8, 1897; Oct. 28, 1897
Colonel Guy V. Henry	Oct. 29, 1897; May 9, 1898
Lieut. Colonel T. A. Baldwin	May 10, 1898; Nov. 21, 1898
Colonel S. M. Whitside	Nov. 22, 1898; May 29, 1902
Lieut. Colonel T. A. Baldwin	May 30, 1902; Oct. 27, 1902
Colonel J. A. Augur	Oct. 28, 1902; Apr. 18, 1909
Lieut. Colonel G. H. G. Gale	Apr. 19, 1909; Sept. 22, 1909
Colonel Thaddeus W. Jones	Sept. 23, 1909; Feb. 28, 1912
Lieut. Colonel and Colonel G. H. G. Gale	Mar. 1, 1912; Oct. 8, 1912
Colonel John C. Gresham	Oct. 9, 1912; July 31, 1914
Colonel Daniel H. Broughton (attached)	Aug. 1, 1914; Aug. 11, 1914
Major G. L. Bryam	Aug. 12, 1914; Sept. 7, 1914
Colonel W. C. Brown	Sept. 8, 1914; May 3, 1916
Major Ellwood W. Evans	May 4, 1916; Aug. 4, 1916
Major Charles Young	Aug. 5, 1916; Aug. 9, 1916
Colonel Ellwood W. Evans	Aug. 10, 1916; Sept. 14, 1916
Lieut. Colonel Charles Young	Sept. 15, 1916; Sept. 28, 1916
Colonel Ellwood W. Evans	Sept. 29, 1916; Feb. 5, 1917
Colonel DeRosey C. Cabell	Feb. 6, 1917; May 23, 1917
Lieut. Colonel Charles Young	May 24, 1917; June 2, 1917
Colonel DeRosey C. Cabell	June 3, 1917; Aug. 21, 1917
Captain George B. Rodney	Aug. 22, 1917; Aug. 25, 1917
Captain Varion D. Dixon	Aug. 26, 1917; Oct. 28, 1917
Captain George B. Rodney	Oct. 29, 1917; Dec. 24, 1917
Colonel DeRosey C. Cabell	Dec. 25, 1917; Dec. 26, 1917
Major George B. Rodney	Dec. 27, 1917; Jan. 25, 1918
Colonel DeRosey C. Cabell	Jan. 26, 1918; Feb. 15, 1918
Lieut. Colonel George B. Rodney	Feb. 16, 1918; Feb. 28, 1918
Colonel Frederick T. Arnold	Mar. 1, 1918; July 10, 1918
Colonel George B. Rodney	July 11, 1918; Oct. 29, 1918
Colonel Cornelius C. Smith	Oct. 30, 1918; Feb. 22, 1919
Colonel William A. Cornell	Feb. 23, 1919; Mar. 28, 1919
Lieut. Colonel Frederick S. Snyder	Mar. 29, 1919; April 12, 1919
Colonel George P. White	April 13, 1919; Aug. 21, 1919
Colonel Guy Carleton	Aug. 22, 1919; Oct. 23, 1919
Colonel George P. White	Oct. 24, 1919; Nov. 13, 1919
Colonel Oren B. Meyer	Nov. 14, 1919; May 1, 1920
Colonel Francis C. Marshall	May 2, 1920; Aug. 3, 1920
Lieut. Colonel Selwyn D. Smith	Aug. 4, 1920; Aug. 22, 1920
Colonel Edwin B. Winans	Aug. 23, 1920—

ROLL OF HONOR

Killed In Action

Sergeant William Christy, Company F, Saline River, Kansas, August 2, 1867.
Private Thomas Smith, Company F, near Fort Hays, Kansas, August 21, 1867.
Wagoner Larkin Foster, Company B, Foster Springs, Texas, September 19, 1871.
Private Clark Young, Company M, Cheyenne Agency, I. T., April 12, 1875.
First Sergeant Charles Butler, Company G, Lake Quemado, Texas, May 4, 1877.
Private Martin Davis, Company C, Eagle Springs, Texas, July 30, 1880.
Private William Tayler, Company F, Camp Safford, Texas, August 4, 1880.
Private Wesley Hardy, Company H, Rattlesnake Springs, Texas, August 6, 1880.
Private George Locks, Company C, Eagle Springs, Texas, August 30, 1880.
Private Carter Burns, Company B, Ojo Caliente, Texas, October 28, 1880.
Private George Mills, Company B, Ojo Caliente, Texas, October 28, 1880.
Corporal William Backers, Company K, Ojo Caliente, Texas, October 28, 1880.
Private J. K. Griffin, Company K, Ojo Caliente, Texas, October 28, 1880.
Private James Stanley, Company K, Ojo Caliente, Texas, October 28, 1880.
Private J. Follis, Troop K, Pinito Mountains, Texas, May 3, 1886.
Sergeant Robert Evans, Troop C, Gaileyville Canyon, A. T., June 3, 1886.
Corporal William L. White, Troop E, Las Guasimas, Cuba, June 24, 1898.
First Lieutenant W. E. Shipp, Tenth Cavalry, San Juan, Cuba, July 1, 1898.
First Lieutenant W. H. Smith, Tenth Cavalry, San Juan, Cuba, July 1, 1898.
Private John H. Smoot, Troop A, San Juan, Cuba, July 1, 1898.
Corporal William F. Johnson, Troop B, San Juan, Cuba, July 1, 1898.
Private John H. Dodson, Troop C, San Juan, Cuba, July 1, 1898.
Private George Stovall, Troop D, San Juan, Cuba, July 1, 1898.
Private Wm. H. Slaughter, Troop G, San Juan, Cuba, July 1, 1898.
Captain Charles T. Boyd, Tenth Cavalry, Carrizal, Mexico, June 21, 1916.
First Lieutenant Henry R. Adair, Tenth Cavalry, Carrizal, Mexico, June 21, 1816.
First Sergeant William Winrow, Troop C, Carrizal, Mexico, June 21, 1916.
Sergeant Will Hines, Troop C, Carrizal, Mexico, June 21, 1916.
Private Thomas Moses, Troop C, Carrizal, Mexico, June 21, 1916.
Horseshoer Lee Talbott, Troop C, Carrizal, Mexico, June 21, 1916.
Private DeWitt Rucker, Troop K, Carrizal, Mexico, June 21, 1916.
Private Charlie Mathews, Troop K, Carrizal, Mexico, June 21, 1916.
Private James E. Day, Troop K, Carrizal, Mexico, June 21, 1916.
Captain Joseph D. Hungerford, Tenth Cavalry, Nogales, Arizona, August 27, 1918.

Engagements of the Regiment

SALINE RIVER, Kansas, August 2, 1867. Co. F. Cheyennes.
Near SALINE RIVER, Kansas, August 21, 1867. Co. F. Cheyennes.
FORT HAYS, Kansas, September 15, 1867. Co. G. Cheyennes.
BIG SANDY CREEK, Kansas, September 15, 1867. Co. I. Cheyennes.
BEAVER CREEK, Kansas, October 18, 1867. Cos. H and I. Comanches.
CAMP SUPPLY, I. T., June 11, 1871. Cos. A, F, H, I and K. Comanches.
DOUBLE MOUNTAIN, I. T., February 5, 1874. Cos. D and G. Comanches.
WICHITA, I. T., August 22-23, 1874. Hqrs., Cos. C, E, H and L. Kiowas and Comanches.
BUFFALO SPRINGS, I. T., April 6, 1875. Co. M. Cheyennes.
SULPHUR SPRINGS, Texas, July 6, 1875. Co. A. Comanches.
SARAGOSSA, Mexico, July 30, 1876. Co. B. Apaches.
PINTO MOUNTAINS, Mexico, August 12, 1876. Cos. B and K. Apaches.
PECOS SPRINGS, Texas, September 13, 1876. Co. G. Comanches.
PECOS RIVER, Texas, October 2, 1876. Co. G. Comanches.
Near FORT GRIFFIN, Texas, May 4, 1877. Co. G. Comanches.
In MEXICO, September 29, 1877. Co. C. Comanches.
SIERRA CANNEL, Mexico, November 29, 1877. Co. B. Alsatti's Apaches.
SALT LAKES, Texas, July 29, 1879. Co. H. Comanches.
PECOS RIVER, Texas, April 2, 1880. Co. L. Comanches.
SHAKEHAND SPRINGS, Texas, April 30, 1880. Co. K. Comanches.
TINAJA DE LAS PALMAS, July 30, 1880. Hqrs. and Band. Apaches.
EAGLE SPRINGS, Texas, July 30, 1880. Cos. C and G. Apaches.
ALAMO SPRINGS, Texas, August 3, 1880. Co. H. Apaches.
Near CAMP SAFFORD, Texas, August 7, 1880. Cos. F and L. Apaches.
RATTLESNAKS SPRINGS, Texas, August 7, 1880. Cos. B, C, G and H. Apaches.
OJO CALIENTE, Texas, October 28, 1880. Co. B. Comanches.
PINTO MOUNTAINS, Mexico, May 3, 1886. Troop G. Geronimo's Apaches.
WHITE MOUNTAINS, Ariz., September 18, 1886. Troop H. Capture of Mangus.
LAS GUASIMAS, Cuba, June 24, 1898. Troops A. B. E and I.
SANTIAGO, Cuba, July 1, 2, 3, 1898. Troops A, B, C, D, E, F, G and I.
CARRIZAL, Mexico, June 21, 1916. Troops C and K.
NOGALES, Arizona, August 27, 1918. Troops A, C and F.

APPENDIX "A."

Brief extracts from the Regimental Returns, selected at random. These short accounts of service on the Old Frontier tell of days that are gone forever, to the sorrow of the old school trooper. The cavalry was the school for courage, daring, endurance.

1868

Company D: Cottonwood Grove, Indian Territory, February 25th. Left Fort Arbuckle for Cottonwood Grove to assist Indian Agent in reclaiming white children held captive by Indians.

1876

Company C: Fort McKavett, Texis. The company returned from scout duty in field against hostiles after absence of six months and seven days.

Company G: Fort Griffin, Texas. Corporal John Robinson and four men pursued Mexican horse thieves, returned November 28, 1876; captured ten Mexicans, fifteen horses. Distance marched 770 miles.

1877

Company A: Private Derwin died July 30th from want of water. Private Gordon died July 31st, being without water for 104 hours. Privates Bond and Isaacs missing since July 30th on account of straggling.

Headquarters: First Lieutenant R. G. Smither, Adjutant, with effective force of Band (16 men), started on scout August 3rd to Bull Creek, Texas, distance of 140 miles in forty-one hours, for relief of Captain Nolan's command which was reported in suffering condition on Staked Plains, men and horses dying from lack of water. Returned to Fort Concho August 14th.

Company F: Camp on the Rio Grande, Texas. Since last report the company has been engaged in scouting after hostile Indians. Distance marched 1500 miles.

January, 1878

Troop H: Station Fort Davis, Texas. Troop left Toleta, Texas, January 18, 1878, where the company had been sent to suppress an insurrection, arrived Fort Davis January 27, 1878. Distance marched 220 miles.

Troop L: Station Fort Concho, Texas. Lieutenant Esterly and ten enlisted men left company January 17, 1878, in pursuit of hostile Indians, returned January 29, 1878. Lieutenant Maxon and twenty-four enlisted men left the post January 18, 1878, in pursuit of hostile Indians, returned January 30, 1878. Distance marched by detachments 350 miles.

February, 1878

Troop F: In the field, camp on Palo Blanco, Texas. Doing patrol and escort duty along the Rio Grande. Distance marched 955 miles.

Company H: Station Fort Davis, Texas. Lieutenant Ayres and twelve enlisted men left company February 17th in pursuit of Indians to Barilla Springs, thence west, returning to post February 19th.

March, 1878

Company H: On March 13, 1878, Captain L. H. Carpenter, Tenth Cavalry; Lieutenant Ayres, and forty enlisted men, left on scout to Russell's ranch, Texas, and adjacent country. Marched to Davis' ranch, Smith's ranch, Ferris' ranch, Presidio and Russel's ranch and scouted up the Rio Grande, returning to Russel's ranch. Distance marched 256 miles.

Company K: The company left Fort Davis, Texas, March 14, 1878, on scout in search of hostile Indians, and proceeded in the direction of the mouth of San Francisco Creek, Texas, southeast of Fort Davis. Distance marched 192 miles.

April, 1878

Company B: Lieutenant John Bigelow, Jr., and twenty-five men left Fort Stockton, Texas, April 15, 1878, in pursuit of hostile Indians, marched a southeast course, returning to post April 24, 1878. Distance marched 350 miles.

Company H: Captain L. H. Carpenter and Second Lieutenant C. G. Ayres, and forty enlisted men, returned from Russel's ranch and vicinity. Distance marched 175 miles.

Company K: The company left Pinto Blanco April 1, 1878, and continued on scout in search of hostile Indians, returning to post April 15, 1878. Distance marched 427 miles. April 21, 1878, a detachment of the company, consisting of one N. C. O and nine privates, under command of Lieutenant Geddes, Twenty-fifth Infantry, left post in search of hostile Indians and returned April 30, 1878. Distance marched 270 miles.

June, 1878

Company B: Lieutenant Beck, with twenty enlisted men, left company on June 29, 1878, in search of parties of Indians who had attacked stage near Pecos Station.

Lieutenant Bigelow and fifteen enlisted men returned to post June 3, 1878, from pursuit of hostile Indians, and left the post June 7, 1878, to watch the approach of marauding Indians from direction of Concho, Texas, returning June 14, 1878. Distance marched by detachments 620 miles.

Company F: Company left Fort Concho, Texas, June 26, 1878, on scout for marauding Indians. No trail found; bad weather during scout causing much suffering to men and horses. Returned to post June 27, 1878. Distance marched 510 miles.

July, 1878

Company B: Lieutenant Beck with twenty enlisted men returned to post July 4, 1878, having been scouting for stage robbers since June 28, 1878.

Company E: Company left San Felipe, Texas, July 25, 1878, on a fresh trail in pursuit of cattle thieves, marched to San Vincente, Mexico, and returned to and recrossed the Rio Grande River into Texas the same day, having captured most of the stolen stock, and returned to post July 26, 1878.

Company K: Captain Lebo and twenty enlisted men left Fort Davis, Texas, July 12, 1878, in pursuit of hostile Indians and returned July 24, 1878. Second Lieutenant Read and ten enlisted men left the company July 7, 1878, in pursuit of hostile Indians and returned July 16, 1878. Distance marched by these detachments 493 miles.

August, 1878

Company E: San Felipe, Texas. The company left post August 15th and crossed the Rio Grande into Mexico in pursuit of Mexican murderers, and returned to post August 18, 1878.

Company G: Fort Sill, I. T. The company left the post on detached service August 11, 1878, per S. O. 174, c. s., Ft. Sill, I. T., to enforce the return of Big Bow (Chief) with his band of Kiowas, and returned with the Indians August 22, 1878. Distance marched 202 miles.

May, 1879

Company A: In the field, Canon Blanco, Texas. Company left Fort Elliott, Texas, May 18, 1879, in pursuit of fugitive Comanche Indians. Distance marched 219 miles.

Company K: Fort Davis, Texas. Second Lieutenant R. D. Read, Jr., left the post May 6, 1879, with a detachment of eight enlisted men in search of hostile Indians. Returned to post May 10, 1879. Distance marched 145 miles.

JOHN J. PERSHING
1ST LIEUT., 10TH CAV.

Company L: In the field, Santa Rosa, Texas. Company scouted from the Pecos toward the Sand Hills, to Victoria Mountains and Seven Springs, Toyah Creek, Ropes Wells, Texas, and crossing Delaware River, N. M.; Black River, N. M.; Seven River, and near the Guadalupe Mountains, back to Santa Rosa, Texas, making three dry camps, which caused several animals to fag somewhat, but not a horse or mule was lost, every man and animal being able to make the same march in three days' less time than was consumed in the present one, without injury to man or beast. Several new crossings on the Pecos River were made. Only a few old signs of Indians were discovered. Distance marched by company and detachments 1426 miles.

JUNE, 1879

Company A The company was in the field since May 18, 1879, in pursuit of fugitive Comanches from Fort Sill, I T

JULY, 1879

Company C In the field, Texas The company has been engaged in scouting and in pursuit of hostile Indians during the month Distance marched by company 1050 miles

AUGUST, 1879

Company H Fort Davis, Texas July 19, 1879, a detachment of twelve men under the command of Captain M L Courtney, Twenty-fifth Infantry on scout from Eagle Springs, Texas, engaged a party of hostile Indians near Salt Lakes Texas, in which fight Corporal William J Webb and Private Geo W Foster, Company H, were wounded, and one horse was killed

SEPTEMBER, 1879

Company B In the field, Texas The company left Camp Santa Rosa, Texas September 17 1879, and scouting in the Sand Hills along the Pecos and over the country between camp and Emigrant Crossing Returned to post September 20th Lieutenant McMartin returned to camp September 7, 1879, with his detachment, having marched 742 miles in pursuit of hostile Indians and recovered twenty-nine stolen horses Distance marched by detachments 963½ miles

MARCH, 1880

Headquarters At the falls of the Pecos River, Texas Colonel B H Grierson commanding District of the Pecos, First Lieutenant R G Smither, A A A G, and detachment of N C S, and Band Tenth Cavalry, left post March 23, 1880, with a view of organizing an expedition consisting of Companies D, E, F, K and L, Tenth Cavalry, and detachment of Twenty-fifth Infantry, as train guard to operate against and to assist in the disarming and dismounting the Mescalero Apache Indians at Mescalero Agency, N M Distance marched 203 miles

APRIL, 1880

Headquarters Near Guadalupe Creek Canon, N M Left Pecos Falls, Texas, April 1st and arrived at Mescalero Agency, N M, April 12, 1880, from the southeast and reported to Colonel Edward Hatch, Ninth Cavalry, commanding District of New Mexico Left the agency April 20th and scouted the Sacramento and Guadalupe Mountains in all directions in a thorough manner Participated in several small skirmishes with the Indians April 2nd, 9th, 16th and 20th, and assisted in the disarming and dismounting of Indians at agency on the 10th, conducting Indian stock to Fort Stanton, and guarding Indian prisoners. Distance marched 564 miles

Company K Sculptured Tanks, Guadalupe Mountains, N M Left Agua Salada Water Holes, Texas, April 1st, arrived at Black River Falls, N M, marched thence northward through the Guadalupe Mountains by way of Guadalupe Creek to the Rio Panasco in the Sacramento Mountains, thence to the agency and took part in the disarming and dismounting the Mescalero Indians April 9th struck the camp of a small party of Mescaleros at Shakehand Springs, N M Killed one buck, captured four squaws and one child, released from captivity a small Mexican boy (Cayetena Segura) aged 11 Captured twenty-one head of horses and mules and destroyed their camp Distance marched 417½ miles

Company L In the field, Gardener's Ranch, N M Lieutenant Esterly and detachment rejoined April 5, 1880, overtook Indians with stolen horses on April 2nd half way between White Sand Hills and Pecos River; wounded one Indian, captured and abandoned eight horses, lost one pack mule, and was forty-eight hours without water. Company arrived at Mescalero Agency April 12th. April 16th took part in affairs against Mescalero Apaches. One Indian supposed to have been killed or wounded; four horses killed, and two horses and three mules captured. Left agency April 20th for Silver Springs on fresh trail overtook party of four or five in number same afternoon and killed one Indian and captured five horses. Distance marched by company 440 miles; detachments 220 miles.

JULY, 1880

Company C: In the field, Texas. Left Fort Davis, Texas, July 25, 1880; arrived at Eagle Springs, Texas, July 29th. Engaged party of hostile Indians on Quitman Road July 30th; lost one man, and five horses killed and one horse and one pack mule wounded. Distance marched 138 miles.

Company G: Eagle Springs, Texas. Left Camp Charlotte, Texas, July 1, 1880, arrived at Fort Stockton, Texas, July 6th. Engaged with hostile Apaches July 30th at Rocky Ridge near Eagle Springs, Texas. Lieutenant Colladay and Private Samuel Prescott wounded, and five horses lost, killed and wounded. Distance marched 333 miles.

AUGUST, 1880

Company A: Near old Fort Quitman, Texas. Left Eagle Springs, Texas, August 2nd and marched to Van Horn's Wells; August 3rd, marched to Devil's Race Course; August 4th, marched to Rattle Snaks Springs; 6th, 7th and 8th, engaged in scouting and picketing the passes of the Sierra Diablo; August 10th, marched to Ash Springs; August 11th, discovered and followed trail of Victoria's band of Apaches from 8 p. m. until 11:45 a. m. of the 10th, when, after marching and reaching the Rio Grande, the pursuit ended by reason of the enemy crossing the river into Mexico. Distance marched by company and detachments 748 miles.

Company F: Camp Safford, Texas. Detachment of company under Sergeant Richardson in action with Indians on August 4th in which Private William Taylor was killed. The detachment being repulsed and driven from their horses, causing the abandonment of some five horses completely caparisoned and equipped, all of which fell into the hands of the Indians. On August 6th, while Captain Kennedy with command was in pursuit of the other Indians, a small party consisting of two bucks and one or two squaws was encountered and in the firing at the Indians which ensued one of the squaws was shot and killed, one pony killed and one taken with command. Distance marched by company and detachments 735 miles.

Company G: Sulphur Water Hole, Texas. Left Eagle Springs, Texas, August 3rd, arrived at Van Horn, Texas, the same night; August 4th, 5th marched to Rattle Snaks Springs, Texas; August 6th engaged with hostile Indians near Rattle Snake Springs. No casualties. August 7th marched to Sulphur Water Hole, Texas. August 3rd Private Julius London, one of a party of scouts, was engaged and wounded in action with hostile Apaches near Eagle Springs, Texas. Distance marched 1256 miles.

Company H: Near Hot Springs, Texas. August 1st engaged in furnishing pickets and scouts from Eagle Springs, Texas. August 3rd Corporal A. Weaver, with Private Brent of H company and a small detail from other companies, while on picket at Alamo Springs discovered Victoria's band of Indians after they had crossed the Rio Grande and had an engagement and running fight for fifteen miles. August 3rd left Eagle Springs in pursuit of Victoria's band; marched to Van Horn and thence to Devil's Race Course, thence across to the Rattle Snake Springs; August 6th participated in an engagement with Victoria's band with Companies B, C and G, under command of Captain L. H. Carpenter, the Indians being repulsed and fleeing to the mountains. Private Wesley Hardy missing in action. Distance marched by company and detachments 1250 miles.

Company K: Near Ojo Caliente, Texas. From August 1st to 7th was engaged in scouting in and about the Sierra Diablo. On learning that Victoria was making at attempt to cross the Rio Grande near Ojo Caliente, August 1st discovered fresh trail of a party of Indians in the Sierra Diablo, followed it about six miles to the eastern slope of the mountains and found their camp, which they had evidently abandoned in great haste, leaving behind a number of ponies and cattle, also a great quantity of slaughtered beef (twelve or fifteen head) which was being prepared for drying, all of which was captured or destroyed. Followed their trail August 2nd and 3rd, finding several ponies and pack mules with their equipment and cargo of fresh beef, etc., abandoned on the trail. The Indians, being on the alert, had taken to flight in due time and made good their escape to the Guadalupe Mountains during the night of the 1st. This was, without doubt, the advance supply camp for Victoria's band of Apaches, who were then making endeavors to reach this point. Distance marched by company and detachments 1442 miles.

SEPTEMBER, 1880

Headquarters: Fort Concho, Texas. Colonel Grierson, with four men of N. C. S. and Band, has been operating in the field against Victoria and his band of Indians since July 10, 1880. They were driven across the Rio Grande twice. In the fight at Tenaja del Las Palomas July 30th Colonel Grierson, his son Robert, Lieutenant Beck and seven men fought about seventy-five Indians.

Company A: During the month the company marched 900 miles.

Company B: During the month the company and detachments marched 1242 miles.

Company H: During the month the company and detachments marched 1281 miles.

Company I: During the month the company and detachments marched 1004 miles.

OCTOBER, 1880

Company B: In the field on Rio Grande below Ojo Caliente, Texas, engaged in patrolling and scouting the Rio Grande. October 28th, before daybreak at Ojo Caliente, while on picket duty Privates Carter Burns and George Mills, with a detachment commanded by Sergeant Charles Perry, were surprised and killed by Indians supposed to be thirty-five or forty strong. Distance marched by company and detachments 1097 miles.

Company E: During the month the company and detachments marched 1480 miles.

Company H: During the month the company and detachments marched 2958 miles.

JANUARY, 1884

Troop M: Pena Colorado, Texas. Saddler Leve Ross mortally wounded, Sergeant Winfield Scott and Private Augustus Dover slightly wounded while under command of Lieutenant Eggleston attempting to arrest a desperado on the military reservation. The desperado, W. A. Alexander, was killed while resisting arrest.

MAY, 1886

Troop K: Pantana, A. T., in the field. Left Calabasas May 1st in pursuit of hostile Indians, and on the 3rd had an engagement with Geronimo's band of hostile Apaches in the Pinto Mountains, Mexico. Killed two bucks, and another supposed to be badly wounded. Private Follis killed, Corporal Scott badly wounded, two horses killed, one wounded and four missing while following the trail. On the 2nd and 3rd the Indians shot and abandoned about thirty head of horses, ponies and mules.

OCTOBER, 1886

Troop H: Fort Apache, A. T. Captain Cooper in command of twenty men of the troop left post on September 14, 1886, and on the 18th found trail of hostile Indians about twenty-five miles east of Thomas Peak of White Mountains, Arizona; pursued them for forty-five miles over a rugged and almost inaccessible country, overtook them and after a running fight of fifteen miles captured the entire band, consisting of Chief Mangus, two bucks, three squaws, two boys, rations, blankets, and everything they possessed, turned over to the C. O., Fort Apache.

APPENDIX "B"

Reports on the action at Las Guasimas, Cuba, June 24, 1898:

CAMP TENTH CAVALRY
Near Santiago de Cuba, June 28, 1898.

The Adjutant General, Second Brigade, Cavalry Division, Fifth Army Corps.

Sir: In connection with the action that took place on the 24th instant at Las Guasimas between troops of the brigade and Spaniards, I have the honor to submit the following, to accompany the reports of the troop commanders of the First Squadron, Tenth Cavalry:

The reports referred to cover the part taken by each organization, and attention is respectfully invited to the same.

As the fight took place under the eyes and direction of the brigade commander, I will only testify to the good and brave conduct of every officer and enlisted man belonging to the four troops of the First Squadron, Tenth Cavalry.

The designations of the troops, together with the names of the officers belonging to the same, who took part in the action, are as follows:

Troop A, Captain William H. Beck and Second Lieutenant F. R. McCoy.
Troop B, Captain J. W. Watson and Second Lieutenant H. O. Williard.
Troop E, Captain C. G. Ayres and Second Lieutenant George Vidmer.
Troop I, First Lieutenant R. J. Fleming and Second Lieutenant A. M. Miller.

Attached to the squadron as medical officer was First Lieutenant L. A. Fuller, Assistant Surgeon, United States Army.

Very respectfully,
S. T. NORVELL,
Major, Tenth Cavalry,
Commanding First Squadron.

In the Field, near Santiago de Cuba, June 27, 1898.

The Adjutant, Tenth Cavalry.

Sir: In obedience to verbal instructions of this date, I report as follows relative to the affair of June 24 with the Spaniards at Las Guasimas:

Shortly after the Hotchkiss guns, under Captain Watson's direction, opened fire upon the Spanish position and the squadron of the First United States Cavalry had been deployed in front of the works occupied by them, I was directed to take my troop (A, Tenth Cavalry) and proceed to the left of Captain Galbraith's troop of the First Cavalry, which was on the left of the First Cavalry Squadron, and support him. This I immediately proceeded to do. I found Captain Galbraith's troop, and after a short consultation with him extended his line with my troop and pushed the line parallel to the hill upon which the Spaniards were located. The First Cavalry Squadron was pushing its line forward in their front. I judged this by their firing. My line was at right angle, approximately, to that of the First Cavalry as I proceeded on the extension of Galbraith's line.

Finding that the hill to the south of that upon which the Spaniards were located was, in my judgment, too far for effective carbine firing, I moved steadily on, deflecting to the right, and proceeding on the southern slope of the hill upon which the Spaniards were entrenched, nearly reaching the summit, when I discovered the First United States Volunteers on my left and communicated with them, stating what troop I commanded. This made the line continuous from the right of the First United States Cavalry Squadron to the left of the First United States Volunteers. I continued my line of march until I reached the summit of the hill upon which the Spaniards were intrenched, to the south and west of their works. I sent Lieutenant McCoy, of my troop, along the ridge to discover if the Spaniards still occupied their works. He returned, reporting that they had left.

While I was proceeding as above stated I heard heavy firing in the direction in which I was pushing, which I ascertained afterwards was the firing occasioned by the attack of the First United States Volunteers upon the Spaniards in their front.

During my entire march I received the fire from the enemy at times, but could not see him, and reached the point at which I was aiming to intercept the Spaniards on their retreat but a few moments after they had fled.

The side of the hill was extremely rough, covered with Spanish daggers, dense chaparral of all kinds, and rocky, making it impossible to see for any distance.

After receiving Mr. McCoy's report I crossed the summit of the hill and marched down the north side, thus completely covering the ground occupied by the Spaniards in our immediate front.

I found toward the eastern part of the summit a wounded man of B Troop, Tenth Cavalry, and a number of stragglers from the First Cavalry, and troops of the Tenth Cavalry, whom I brought in.

I will add that the enlisted men of A Troop, Tenth Cavalry, behaved well, silently and alertly obeying orders, and without becoming excited when the fire of the enemy reached them.

I am, sir, very respectfully, your obedient servant,

WM. H. BECK,
Captain, Tenth Cavalry, Commanding Troop A.

Sevilla, Santiago de Cuba, June 27, 1898.
The Adjutant, Tenth United States Cavalry, Headquarters of Regiment in Field.

Sir: I have the honor to submit the following report:

At about 7:15 to 7:20 a. m., June 24, 1898, Troop B, Tenth Cavalry, was marching along the road or trail, leading from Altares to Santiago de Cuba. A few minutes after I heard several shots, and directly the squadron of the Tenth Cavalry was halted, my troop being about twenty yards from a little creek directly in front and thick brush on the left, the right being slightly more open. About this time a volley from the Spanish was fired; the first I heard at about 7:30 a. m., I should judge. I cautioned the men to lie down on the left side of the road and keep in the shelter as much as possible. A few minutes after this Troop A, Tenth Cavalry, was ordered to the left of the line, and I was ordered by Major Norvell, Tenth Cavalry, to report to Brigadier General Young, U. S. Volunteers, for instructions. I did so immediately. The general was standing in a most exposed position, about thirty to forty yards beyond the creek already spoken of, slightly in rear of the Hotchkiss gun battery. The general ordered me to move my troop out in the extreme right at once, prolonging the line of the First United States Cavalry, already there. I ordered the troop forward at once, telling them to take advantage of all cover available. In the meantime the volleys from the Spanish were coming in quite frequently and striking the ground on all sides near where we were. I found it very difficult to move the men forward after having found cover, and ran back to a portion of the troop near an old brick wall, and ordered them forward at once. They then made a dash forward, and in doing so three or four men were wounded, Private Russel severely. Who the others were I do not know. We encountered a severe fire directly after this move forward, and Private Wheeler was wounded in the left leg. There was a wire fence on our right, and such thick underbrush that we were unable to get through right there, so had to follow along the fence for some distance before being able to penetrate. Finally, was able to get the greater portion of my men through, and about this time I met Lieutenants Fleming and Miller, Tenth Cavalry, moving through the thicket on my left. I there heard the order passed on "not to fire ahead," as there was danger of firing into our own forces. In the meantime there was shouting from the First Cavalry in our front, "Don't fire on us in the rear." My troop had not fired a shot to my knowledge, nor the knowledge of any non-commissioned officers in the troop. About this time I found I was unable to keep the troop deployed, as they would huddle up behind one rock or tree, so I gave all sergeants orders to move out on the extreme right and to keep in touch with those on their left.

Then, with a squad of about five men, I moved to the right front, and was unfortunate enough to lose the troop, i. e., I could see nothing of them except the men with me. But as I had given explicit instructions to my sergeants, in case I was lost from them, to continue to advance until halted by some one in authority, I moved ahead myself, hoping to find them later on. In making a rush forward three men of my squad were lost from me in some way. I still had two men with me, Privates Combs and Jackson, and in the next advance made I picked up a First Cavalry sergeant who had fallen out from exhaustion. After a terrible climb up the ridge in front of me, and a very regular though effective fire from the enemy kept up until we were about sixty yards from the summit of hill, we reached the advance line of the First United States Cavalry, under command of Captain Wainwright. I then reported to him for orders, and moved forward when he next advanced. The firing had ceased, and no more shots were fired, to my knowledge, after this time. With the First Cavalry, Troop G, we followed along the right of the ridge and down to the right front, encountering no opposition or fire from the enemy, but finding the enemy's breastworks in confusion, ammunition and articles of clothing scattered around; also one dead Spaniard and two Mauser rifles. At the foot of the ridge we met some of the First Volunteer Cavalry, and, being utterly exhausted, I was obliged to lie down. Soon after, Captain Mills, Adjutant General of the Second Brigade, Cavalry Division, came up to where I was and placed me in command of Troop K, First United States Cavalry, whose officers were wounded. I then marched them forward on the road to where General Wheeler was sitting, and received orders from Colonel Wood, First Volunteer Cavalry, to remain until further orders and make no further advance. Directly afterwards, learing the action was over, I reported back to General Young, and received orders to remain camped with the First Cavalry Squadron, where the action had closed. In the meantime, I should have stated that I had found the principal part of my troop, and collected them and left them under the first sergeant, when I went back to receive orders. So far as I know, and to the best of my knowledge, the men of my troop acted with the greatest bravery, advancing on an enemy who could not be seen, and subjected to a severe and heavy fire at each step, which was only rendered ineffective to a great degree by the poor marksmanship of the enemy, as many times we were in sight of them, (I discovered this by observation after the engagement), while we could see nothing. We were also subjected to a severe reverse fire from the hills in our right rear, several men being wounded by this fire. Throughout the fight the men acted with exceptional coolness, in my judgment.

The casualties were: Privates Russell, Braxton, and Morris, severely wounded; Privates F. A. Miller, Grice, Wheeler, and Gaines, slightly wounded, i. e., less severely. None killed.

Very respectfully,
HARRY O. WILLIARD,
Second Lieutenant, Tenth United States Cavalry, Commanding Troop B, Tenth Cavalry, during action near Las Guasimas, June 24, 1898.

The Assistant Adjutant General, Young's Brigade. (Through Squadron Commander).

Sir: I have the honor to report that on the 24th instant two commissioned officers and fifty-three enlisted men of Troop E, Tenth Cavalry, went into action, with other troops of the brigade, against the regular Spanish infantry, and were placed by General Young in person in support of Captain J. W. Watson's (Tenth Cavalry), two Hotchkiss guns, and also to support the troops in our front should they need it. The position of the troop was in plain view of the Spaniards, who occupied a high ridge and had the exact range; but pursuant to their instructions they held their positions one hour and a quarter without firing a shot, for fear of firing upon our own men. Their coolness and fine discipline were superb.

In connection herewith, it gives me great pleasure to call attention to the great gallantry of Second Lieutenant George Vidmer, Tenth Cavalry, and Privates Burr Neal, W. B. Nelson, Augustus Wally, and A. C. White, who, under a very heavy fire, came to my assistance in carrying Major Bell, First Cavalry, to a place of safety, he being shot through the leg below the knee and his leg broken.

Very respectfully, your obedient servant,
CHARLES G. AYERS,
Captain, Tenth Cavalry, Commanding Troop E.

One corporal, W. S. White, killed, and Trumpeter W. H. Johnson slightly wounded.
C. G. AYRES,
Captain Tenth Cavalry.

Second Brigade, Cavalry Division.
(Through Military Channels.)

Sir: I have the honor to submit the following report of the operations of Troop I, Tenth Cavalry, under my command in the action of the 24th of June:

Strength of troop: Officers—First Lieutenant R. J. Fleming, Tenth Cavalry, commanding Troop I; Second Lieutenant A. M. Miller, Tenth Cavalry. Enlisted men—Sergeants, 7; corporals, 6; privates, 37; total, 50. Aggregate, 52.

The troop was on road leading out into space where action commenced, and was the third troop in the Tenth Cavalry Squadron. In this position the troop was well protected by high banks on either side of the road. I heard an order from the brigade commander to the squadron commander, Major Norvell, to send forward two troops of the Tenth Cavalry. Not knowing that Captain Beck's troop had already gone forward, I did not immediately move out, until B troop, in my front, had gone about thirty yards. Then the squadron commander informed me that I should also go forward. I moved out, with troop inclined to the right, into the thick underbrush on the right of road, then moved forward until left of my troop rested against old fence where the hospital was afterwards placed. In this movement to the right I passed beyond B troop, which I found posted just as I entered woods on right of road. This troop, as we moved forward, inclined to the right, and during the remainder of action was on my right. Up to this time I had no knowledge of the position of the enemy.

While the troop was in this position, with left against wooden fence, I moved out into the open space on the left and met Major Bell, First Cavalry, who informed me that the First Cavalry was in front of my left and cautioned me not to fire to the front. By this time I discovered that the enemy was posted on the high ridge immediately in front and to the right. I moved back to the troop, moved them to the right so as to uncover the First Cavalry as much as possible, and then moved directly for the hill, seeking cover wherever possible, and advancing on the run across open spaces. On account of not knowing the position of First Cavalry my men were cautioned not to fire unless by order of an officer. After arriving at the steep part of the ridge the ascent was very difficult. The underbrush was impenetrable in most places, the side of the ridge being covered, in addition, by thick prickly weed, through which paths had always to be cut with knives and sabers.

In only two cases did I see any of the enemy, when I allowed part of my men to halt and fire; but with these two exceptions we advanced steadily, as the cover was perfect. The advance, however, was very slow owing to the difficulty of getting through. Just before we struck the first fortification of the Spaniards the left of my line caught up with the right of Captain Wainwright's troop of the First, under command of Lieutenant Whitman, who reached the top of the hill immediately before my troop. I passed along the top of the ridge until I reached the descent on the other end. The detachment of First Cavalry passed down and joined the troop, and I posted outposts on the ridge in order to protect the right of our line in the valley below.

Shortly after Colonel Wood of the First Volunteer Cavalry came to my position and ordered me to establish outposts. When he learned I had already done so he told me to remain until relieved. I was relieved shortly after, but remained in position until 3:30 p. m., when I marched back to camp.

Three men (privates) were wounded in troop, all while in position near wooden fence at commencement of advance.

Wounded—Kelley Mayberry, Amos B. Reed, sent to hospital ship; Wesley Jones, shot in hand, but remained during the fight; slight wound.

The entire troop behaved with great coolness and obeyed every order. Owing to the underbrush it was impossible for me to see but very few men at a time, but as they all arrived on the crest about the time I did, or shortly after, they certainly advanced steadily.

I would especially like to mention the conduct of three men who were under my personal observation: Farrier Sherman Harris, for unusual coolness and gallantry. He kept in advance and picked out the best cover for the men in his immediate rear. Wagoner John Boland, for coolness in action. I think he killed the Spaniard found on the crest, as we could see one man standing behind tree about four hundred yards from us, and Boland coolly fixed his sight and took careful aim and fired, although the bullets were falling very thickly around us, as the enemy had apparently discovered our position. Immediately after he fired the Spaniard either jumped or fell, but he looked as though he fell. Boland remained there until the firing ceased. Private Elsie Jones, for unusual coolness and gallantry. He has been only two months in the service, but behaved like a veteran. I would also like to mention the conduct of Second Lieutenant A. M. Miller, of my troop. He displayed great coolness and gallantry and used the best judgment in directing the movements of the men under his command.

Very respectfully, your obedient servant,

R. J. FLEMING,
First Lieutenant, Tenth Cavalry, Commanding Troop.

TROOP B, TENTH CAVALRY

Six Miles from Santiago, Cuba, June 27, 1898.

Adjutant, Tenth Cavalry.

Sir: I have the honor to submit the following report of part taken in the engagement on the 24th instant by the Tenth Cavalry detachment temporarily in charge of four Hotchkiss mountain guns:

I put the guns in position under the personal direction of the brigade commander. The distance was estimated at 1000 yards. This being found a little high, the sights were lowered to 900 yards and kept at that range during the engagement. Great difficulty was experienced in observing the effect of the shots, owing to the smoke, which hung in front of them, and the brush on each side, but two of the first 900 yards were seen to go to the right spot, and it was presumed the others were going right. The shells were used sparingly, as I could bring only one box (fifty rounds) of ammunition. Twenty-two shots were fired. The fire was directed mainly at a rock fortifications held by the Spaniards, but sometimes at a thick clump of bushes on a high point near the fortification. In looking over this part of the field after the fight I found where three shells had struck; one had struck the center of the rock fort, another had cut off a small tree 18 inches above the top of the fort, a third had exploded 20 feet in front of a line of ten or twelve Spaniards (as shown by the line of empty cartridge shells which they used). Nearly all the others undoubtedly struck in the near vicinity of these three, and it is hoped contributed to the success of the day.

Casualties—Corporal Love, Troop B, left arm grazed by bullet; Private Gaines, same troop, shot in finger, left hand.

Corporal W. F. Johnson, Troop B, deserves special mention for his efficiency and perfect coolness under fire. He was non-commissioned officer in charge, and the Hotchkiss battery was, apparently, on account of the smoke from it, a special target for the enemy's fire.

Respectfully submitted,

J. W. WATSON,
Captain Tenth Cavalry, Temporarily Commanding Battery.

APPENDIX "C"

The following report was submitted through channels, recommending Sergeant Graham for gallantry:

Fort Leavenworth, Kansas, 5th of January, 1899

Captain Charles Ayres, Tenth Cavalry, Huntsville, Alabama

Sir I have the honor to submit to you the following remarks concerning the service of Sergeant John Graham, of your troop, who was detailed by you for temporary duty with gatling guns under my command at the battle of the 1st of July, 1898, with a view that the same may be forwarded with the soldier's record, and such recommendations as you may care to make, by way of his regimental headquarters for consideration by the board of officers appointed at Washington to consider meritorious services during the Spanish-American war

Sergeant Graham particularly distinguished himself by coolness and courage about sundown on July 1st, at a time when the gatling battery, with which he was serving, had become a target for the Spanish artillery fire He rendered particularly valuable service in keeping the ammunition supply up at this time, and at one time, when a shell was about to explode in the battery, endeavored to shield his commanding officer, myself, with his own body His services at this time, in keeping the ammunition going, were particularly dangerous as it had to be carried some distance exposed to the view and fire of the enemy, but he so well performed this work that the gatlings were enabled to drive the enemy's gunners away from their guns by directing a steady and continuous fire upon their pieces

For these distinguished services it is my opinion that Sergeant Graham should receive the Medal of Honor, and I respectfully ask that you concur in such recommendation, and cause this to be forwarded with suitable remarks for the action of the proper board of officers

Very respectfully,

(Signed) JOHN H PARKER,
First Lieutenant, Thirteenth Infantry.

Late commanding Gatling Gun Detachment, Fifth Army Corps.

First endorsement on L R No 45, dated January 10, 1898, relative to recommendation of Sergeant John Graham, Troop E, Tenth Cavalry, for Medal of Honor, by Lieutenant John Parker, First Lieutenant, Thirteenth Infantry

CAMP OF TENTH CAVALRY

Huntsville, Ala , January 10, 1899

Respectfully forwarded to the Adjutant General, U S Army, through regimental headquarters

I saw this sergeant while on duty with this gatling gun battery July 1st at sundown, and I know that there was no more daring man in Cuba, and for endeavoring to shield his commanding officer, Lieutenant Parker, by trying to cover him with his own body to prevent an exploding shell from striking him he is under the law entitled to the Medal of Honor.

(Signed) CHARLES G AYRES,
Captain Tenth Cavalry, Commanding Troop E

A true copy , S D Rockenbach, First Lieutenant, Tenth Cavalry, Adjutant

APPENDIX "D"

Report of Lieutenant Colonel T. A. Baldwin on the Battle of Santiago:

HEADQUARTERS TENTH U. S. CAVALRY

Before Santiago de Cuba, July 8, 1898.

The Adjutant General, Second Brigade, Cavalry Division.

Sir: I have the honor to submit the following report of the part taken by the Tenth U. S. Cavalry in the battle of July 1st, 2nd and 3rd, 1898, before Santiago de Cuba:

On the morning of July 1st the regiment, consisting of Troops A, B, C, D, E, F, G and I, and Field and Staff, occupied a position on the left of the Second Brigade, Cavalry Division, this line extending nearly north and south on a ridge some three or four miles from Santiago. At about 6:30 a. m., a battery of artillery posted a short distance from my right opened fire upon the works of Santiago, the regiment being exposed to much of the return fire of the enemy's batteries. After the artillery firing had ceased the regiment moved to the right, passed the sugar mill, and proceeded in rear of the brigade down the road leading towards Santiago. The movement was delayed as we approached the San Juan River and the regiment came within the range of fire about one-half mile from the crossing. Upon reaching the river I found that the Seventy-first New York Volunteers were at the crossing and that the regiment preceding mine had a converging artillery and infantry fire from the three block houses and entrenchments in front, and the works further to the left and nearer to Santiago. This fire was probably drawn by a balloon which preceded the regiment to a point near the ford, where it was held. I was directed to take a position to the right behind the river bank for protection. While moving to this position, and while there, the regiment suffered considerable loss. After an interval of twenty or thirty minutes, I was directed to form line of battle in a partially open field, facing toward the block houses and strong entrenchments to the north occupied by the enemy. Much difficulty was found on account of the dense undergrowth, crossed in several directions by wire fences. As a part of the cavalry division under General Sumner, the regiment was formed in two lines, the first squadron under Major S. T. Norvell, consisting of Troops A, B, E and I leading; the second line under Major T. J. Wint, consisting of Troops C, F, G. Troop D, having crossed further down the river, attached itself to a command of infantry and moved with that command on the two block houses. The regiment advanced in this formation under a heavy converging fire from the enemy's position, proceeding but a short distance when the two lines were united into one. The advance was rapidly continued in an irregular line toward the block houses and entrenchments to the right front. During this advance the line passed some troops of the First Cavalry, which I think had previously been formed on our right.

Several losses occurred before reaching the top of the hill, First Lieutenant Wm. H. Smith being killed as he arrived on its crest.

The enemy having retreated toward the northwest, the second and third block houses, new lines were formed and a rapid advance was made upon these new positions. The regiment assisted in capturing these works from the enemy and, with the exception of Troops C and D who in the meantime had joined the First Volunteer Cavalry, then took up a position to the north of the second block house, remaining there during the night. With some changes in the position of troops they held this line on the 2nd and 3rd under a very heavy and continuous fire from the enemy's entrenchments in front, and the regiment now occupies a part of the most advanced entrenched position. Some troops lost their relative positions in line during the first day of the battle, but attached themselves to others and continued to move forward. During the entire engagement the regiment acted with extraordinary coolness and bravery. It held its position at the ford and moved forward unflinchingly after deployment through the dense brush under the heavy fire from the enemy's works.

The officers and men in general throughout exhibited great bravery, obeying orders with unflinching alacrity while attacking with small arms an enemy strongly posted in entrenchments and block houses and supported by artillery. Words cannot express my gratification at such conduct, and I would request that such service receive some special recognition. It is difficult to distinguish between officers and men, all of whom are so deserving, but of the officers whose conduct on the field came under my direct personal observation, I would especially mention Major S. T. Norvell and Major T. J. Wint, squadron commanders, First Lieutenant John J Pershing, quartermaster, First Lieutenant M H Barnum, adjutant, for their untiring energy, faithfulness and gallantry during this engagement, and would recommend the officers named for brevet commissions

I desire to recommend the following medical officers, attached to the Tenth U S Cavalry Captain, Assistant Surgeon M M Brown, First Lieutenant, Assistant Surgeon L A Fuller, for their untiring zeal and fearless energy in their attendance under fire of wounded officers and men of my own and other commands during the entire day of July 1st and succeeding days of the engagement

I would invite attention to the following list of men especially recommended in the enclosed reports forwarded herewith:

Troop A—Corporal Jno Anderson and Private R A Parker
Troop C—First Sergeant Adam Houston
Troop E—First Sergeant Peter McCann; Sergeants Benj Fasit, Ozran Gaither and Wm Payne, and Corporal Thos. E Herbert
Troop I—Private Elsie Jones, previously recommended

Very respectfully, your obedient servant,
(Signed) T A BALDWIN,
Lieutenant Colonel, Tenth Cavalry, Commanding Regiment

HEADQUARTERS TENTH CAVALRY
Near Santiago de Cuba, July 8th, 1898

To the Adjutant General, Second Brigade, Cavalry Division

Sir · I have the honor to state that owing to my desire to submit my report of the actions taken part in by my regiment on July 1st, 2nd and 3rd at San Juan, Cuba, at as early date as possible under the instructions received, I was unable to make a complete report on the 6th inst, and therefore submit this supplementary report of the actions referred to

After a thorough investigation of the conduct of the officers of my regiment in the battle of the 1st inst, and the actions of the 2nd and part of the 3rd, I make recommendations that the following named officers be brevetted to the highest rank which the War Department may deem proper to bestow in each case or honorably mentioned

Captain Wm H Beck, Tenth Cavalry, for conspicuous gallantry, good judgment, and endurance I urgently and respectfully recommend him for a brevet

Captain T W Jones Tenth Cavalry For conspicuous gallantry, good judgment, and endurance I urgently and respectfully recommend him for a brevet

Captain Chas G Ayres, Tenth Cavalry, For conspicuous gallantry, good judgment, and endurance I urgently and respectfully recommend him for a brevet.

Captain J W Watson, Tenth Cavalry For conspicuous gallantry, good judgment, and endurance I urgently and respectfully recommend him for honorable mention

Captain John Bigelow. I earnestly and respectfully recommend him for honorable mention

First Lieutenant J B Huges For conspicuous gallantry and endurance
First Lieutenant R L Livermore. For conspicuous gallantry and endurance
First Lieutenant E D Anderson For conspicuous gallantry and endurance
First Lieutenant R I Fleming For conspicuous gallantry and endurance
Second Lieutenant Geo Vidmer For conspicuous gallantry and endurance
Second Lieutenant A M Miller. For conspicuous gallantry and endurance
Second Lieutenant H O Willard For conspicuous gallantry and endurance
Second Lieutenant H C Whitehead For conspicuous gallantry and endurance
Second Lieutenant F R McCoy For conspicuous gallantry and endurance
Second Lieutenant T. A Roberts For conspicuous gallantry and endurance.
Second Lieutenant A E Kennington For conspicuous gallantry and endurance

I make these recommendations as in each individual case the gallantry displayed in leading men to the assault of entrenched works who were armed with the carbine and which works were defended by men armed with the Mauser rifle who used them well prevents any possible question as to the term applied

I feel that if there is any further recognition which can be bestowed upon the officers named it should be done, and I have recommended them for a brevet only because I do not know what additional honor can be given them at this time by the Government for their splendid conduct by which they have shown not only high courage but their ability to command men upon the field of battle.

Very respectfully, your obedient servant,
(Signed) T. A. BALDWIN,
Lieutenant Colonel, Tenth Cavalry, Commanding Regiment.

Report by Major Norvell, including his troop commanders, on the Battle of Santiago, July 1, 2, 3, 1898.

Before Santiago de Cuba, July 5, 1898.

Adjutant, Tenth United States Cavalry.

Sir: The following is a report of the part taken by the First Squadron, Tenth Cavalry, consisting of Troops A, B, E and I, in action with the Spaniards on the 1st, 2nd and 3rd instant:

On the evening of June 30th the regiment, as a part of the Second Brigade, Cavalry Division, took position on the extreme left of the line, about five miles from Santiago.

On the morning of the 1st, after an artillery duel of short duration between Grimes's battery and the artillery of the enemy, the regiment moved forward toward the town to the crossing of the San Juan River, when it immediately became engaged. The regiment took position in a wood, and here suffered considerable loss, due to the fact that the whole of the enemy's fire appeared to be directed to this point. In a short time we moved out of the wood by the right flank and then deployed to the left, being then directly in front of the enemy and about one mile distant from his works, marked by three houses about half a mile from one another. The enemy were strongly entrenched in front of these houses. The line, consisting of the cavalry division, under direction of Brigadier General Sumner, moved forward in double time, under a terrific fire of the enemy. We had a very heavy jungle to march through, besides the river (San Juan) to cross, and during our progress many men were killed and wounded. The troops became separated from one another, though the general line was pretty well preserved. The works of the enemy were carried in succession by the troops and the Spaniards were steadily driven back toward the town to their last ditches. We now found ourselves about half a mile from the city, but the troops being by this time nearly exhausted, here entrenched themselves for the night under fire. By dark this line was occupied by all the troops engaged during the day.

July 2 we changed our position to about 600 yards to the right, and were under a heavy fire during the whole day until dark, when we were again changed to about half a mile to the right and a little nearer to the works of the enemy.

July 2 and until noon we were engaged with the enemy. At noon firing was suspended on both sides by reason of a flag of truce being sent forward, presumably to give notice of the bombardment of the city.

The conduct of the officers and enlisted men of my squadron was simply superb.

The following is a list of the killed and wounded: Killed—Troop A, Private John H. Smart; Troop B, Corporal William P. Johnson. Wounded—Troop A, First Lieutenant R. L. Livermore, Second Lieutenant F. R. McCoy, Sergeant Smith Johnson, Corporal Joseph C. Mitchell, Trumpeter Nathan Wyatt, Privates William A. Cooper, Benjamin Franklin, Wiley Hipsher, Richard James, Daniel Blue. All July 1. July 2, Private Luther D. Gould. July 3. William H. Brown. Troop B. July 1, Privates John Prim and William Gregory; July 2. Second Lieutenant Harry O. Williard. Missing—Saddler John H. Ubanks, George Berry and William Jackson. Troop E, July 1. Sergeant William Payne, Blacksmith Lewis L. Anderson; Privates Henry McCormick, Gilmore Givens, Hilly Brown. Troop I, July 1. First Sergeant Robert Millbrown, Sergeant W. G. Gunter, Privates Frank D. Bennett, Thornton Berkley, Thomas H. Hardy, Wesley Jones, Houston Riddle. Missing—Private John F. Chinn.

Respectfully submitted,
S. T. NORVELL,
Major, Tenth Cavalry, Commanding First Squadron.

TROOP A, TENTH CAVALRY

Near Santiago, July 5, 1898.

The Adjutant, Tenth Cavalry.

Sir: I have the honor to report, in accordance with instructions from your office of this date, the following relative to the part taken by Troop A, Tenth Cavalry, in the actions against the Spaniards of July 1, 2 and 3, 1898:

On the morning of July 1 the troop formed part of the support to a battery of artillery on the extreme front of the line of troops. After the battery removed from the action the troop was ordered out on the road leading toward Santiago and in the direction of the entrenchments and block houses occupied by the Spaniards. The troop was on the right of the First Squadron, Tenth Cavalry. After proceeding for probably a mile and a half, the latter part of which march was under heavy fire from the enemy, the troop was directed to take its place in line on the left of the First United States Cavalry. In accomplishing this the troop passed under a heavy fire of shell and of musketry. Shortly after this formation the troop, in connection with the others on its right and left, was ordered to change its front and move in line against the Spanish block houses. The fire from the enemy at this time was very heavy. I had lost two men wounded in forming line upon the creek bank, and in this movement forward the troop was much impeded by heavy thickets and dense chaparral. The rush forward was continued within intermission. A portion of the right platoon, under Lieutenant Livermore, became separated in one of the thickets, and under instructions received personally from the brigadier general commanding, continued up the slope toward his right and toward the first block house. The balance of the troop, with Lieutenant McCoy and myself, also moved in that direction, but, observing that a large number of troops had succeeded in reaching the slope on account of their shorter line, I continued my march at a rapid gait to a point nearer the second block house, swinging the troop in a diagonal direction and advancing, firing, and receiving fire, until I reached the summit of the hills between the second and third block houses. Upon this crest I was directed by an aide of the brigadier general commanding to hold the ridge. At this juncture Lieutenant Livermore arrived, having come by way of block house No. 1. During his march he had been subjected to a heavy fire, losing several men wounded.

The troop held the crest referred to for about an hour, at times being subjected to an extremely heavy fire from about 150 Spaniards, who were in line in front of their barracks, and others in the timber who had retreated from the block houses and were continuing the fight. The fire at one time became so heavy and the line of Spaniards appeared so regular that I was apprehensive that my force might be too small to hold the ridge. Lieutenant H. G. Lyon, Twenty-fourth Infantry, appeared at this juncture and offered to submit himself to my orders. I had just previously discovered Lieutenant J. B. Hughes' Hotchkiss Mountain Battery approaching the position. I requested him to place one of his guns in action, which he promptly did. Lieutenant Lyons forming on the left of the gun and opening fire, A Troop being on the right of the gun. I held the position until the arrival of a light battery and other troops, among them the Seventy-first New York, when I placed my men parallel to the position on the opposite side of the road, and in contact with the squadron of the Tenth Cavalry, to which I belonged, which had in the meantime arrived at that point. During this time Lieutenant F. R. McCoy was severely wounded while actively directing the fire of this platoon. I had lost, up to this time, one enlisted man killed, and several wounded. While in the position above referred to, and in contact with the squadron, the troop lying below the ridge, Major Wint directed that the crest be occupied, as the enemy had increased his fire on our lines. Troop A immediately moved forward and opened fire, having one man wounded at this point, and one man killed in the line, a straggler from the infantry. The fire ceased about dark and the troop lay under arms in its place under the hill. A detail from the troop assisted in building earthworks during the night.

On the morning of July 2 the troop moved with the squadron up into the rifle pits, a short distance to the right of the previous position, where details from the troop engaged the enemy during the entire day, one man of the troop being wounded while in the rifle pits. On the evening of the 2nd the troops moved to a point still farther to the right, assisting in digging rifle pits within 500 yards of the advanced works of the enemy. During the 3rd the firing between the lines of rifle pits was continuous until about noon. The troop is now occupying this position.

During the series of close fights on the 1st, and in the engagements in the rifle pits up to the 3rd at noon, the troop lost one officer wounded, one enlisted man killed, and eleven enlisted men wounded.

I respectfully invite attention of the regimental commander to the fact that, in my judgment, the conduct of the officers of Troop A, First Lieutenant R. L. Livermore and Second Lieutenant F. R. McCoy, could not be surpassed for coolness and the skillful performance of duty under heavy fire, and I recommend that proper recognition of their gallant service be bestowed by proper authority. The behavior of the enlisted men was magnificent, paying studious attention to orders while on the firing line, and generally exhibiting an intrepidity which marks the first-class soldier.

Very respectfully, your obedient servant,
WM. H. BECK,
Captain, Tenth Cavalry, Commanding Troop A.

TROOP B, TENTH CAVALRY
One mile from Santiago de Cuba, July 5, 1898.

The Adjutant, Tenth Cavalry.

Sir: I have the honor to report the part taken by B Troop in actions of the 1st, 2nd and 3rd instant:

B Troop was on right and advanced as skirmishers, guide center. Being informed by General Sumner that the objective was the house ahead, I advanced by two rushes and then double time. The country advanced over was covered with thick brush, and on emerging in the open near the house I could find only seven men of the troop. With these I advanced to the house, arriving in rear of and along with Colonel Victor's line, which I found deployed in front of mine on beginning the advance. Without stopping, I followed with the seven men of my troop the retreating enemy to the most advanced position occupied at this present time. After helping to hold this position an hour or so, I went back, as soon as it was reinforced, to find my troop. On 2nd and 3rd my troop, with others, held the position gained. Casualties: One officer wounded, one corporal killed, two privates wounded.

Very respectfully,
J. W. WATSON,
Captain, Tenth Cavalry, Commanding Troop.

July 5, 1898.
Report of operations of Troop I, Tenth Cavalry, on July 1, 2 and 3, 1898:
Adjutant General, Second Brigade, Cavalry Division.

About 3:30 p. m., June 30, 1898, troop received orders to move. About 4:00 p. m. troop started with regiment, but owing to delay did not get into position until after dark. Troop bivouacked alongside of road with regiment. Remained there during bombardment of next morning. Returned with regiment; left packs alongside of road under charge of guard, and lay down under such cover as possible. Two men in troop were wounded here while troop was marching along road. Troop remained here about five minutes, when I received orders to move to right of road. We moved to the right, crossed creek, and moved alongside of creek to fairly good cover. Remained here for about half an hour, exposed to a pretty heavy artillery fire. Then received orders to move forward and form skirmish line on edge of creek, perpendicular to last position. Troop moved forward from this position by successive movements until the second creek was reached, when troop moved to right and crossed creek. The left of troop, under command of Lieutenant A. M. Miller, moved directly up the hill and participated in attack on block house on right of enemy's position. This part, under Lieutenant Miller, afterwards crossed the valley between the block houses and was in the attack on the block house on left of enemy's position. It then moved forward with the First Regular Cavalry and First Volunteer Cavalry until it reached the position now held by First Volunteer Cavalry, the latter being on left and regular cavalry on right. The right of troop, under my command, passed creek, bore to right, crossed fence into road, and moved down road about thirty yards, crossed through fence; from this position advanced through swampy ground to right of pond directly on trench between two block houses. In this charge the troop had caught up with preceding troops and was well up to the front. Troop occupied ground in front of this trench and fired volleys at enemy's next line of entrenchments, while the nemy was manning them. Troop then advanced through wire fence, and advanced to extreme edge of hill, now occupied by entrenchments of First Volunteer Cavalry. There was First Volunteer Cavalry and Tenth Cavalry in this position—in all, about one hundred men. Lieutenant Anderson. of the Tenth Cavalry, here joined me. Remained here about an hour, when was informed line was being formed in the rear. Went back and formed on left of First Volunteer Cavalry. Troop assisted in digging trenches that night.

July 2. Part of troop in trenches; remainder about twenty yards in rear until about 2 p. m., when it was ordered down to base of hill. Men in trenches relieved at 6 p. m. At night attack troop formed line, under orders, near crest of hill, near position in camp.

July 3. Remained in camp until 3 p. m., when troop was ordered to right and joined rest of regiment.

Losses: Wounded—First Sergeant Robert Millbrown, Sergeant Gunter, Private Bennett, Private Burkley, Private Hardy, Private Wesley Jones, Private Riddell. Missing— Private J. F. Chinn, Jr.

The entire troop behaved with great gallantry. I have no special recommendation to make. One recruit, Private Elsie Jones, particularly distinguished himself. I have recommended him before, in fight of June 2.

Lieutenant Miller conducted himself with great coolness and used good judgment in giving orders.

Very respectfully,
R. J. FLEMING,
First Lieutenant, Tenth Cavalry, Commanding Troop I.

Reports of Major Wint and his troop commanders on the Battle of Santiago, July 1, 2, 3, 1898.

Philadelphia, Nov. 28th, 1898.

The Adjutant, Tenth Cavalry, Huntsville, Ala.

In compliance with your request of the 22nd inst., I have the honor to submit the following report of the action of Second Squadron, Tenth Cavalry—Troops C, D, F and G— on July 1st, 1898, at San Juan Hill:

The Second Squadron, following the First, marched to near crossing of the creek at foot of hills, where, after a short halt, packs were deposited and the marching continued to crossing, and then up creek about seventy-five yards, where the troops were placed under the best shelter to be found, but which was not sufficient to prevent quite a heavy loss from the enemy's fire, which opened immediately after the packs were deposited, and was quite heavy during the march, and for half an hour after taking a new position.

Upon halting, I found one of my troops, Troop D, absent, and reported its absence to the Regimental Commander, who sent his staff officer and others to find it, but without success. At about 2 p. m. the second squadron was formed in support of first squadron, and advanced in direction of Sugar House Ridge between the two block houses, keeping a distance of twenty-five yards in rear of first squadron. After advancing a short distance, came in view of troops to our right front at sugar house, and on left front troops were advancing on block house. From this point a strip of thick woods continued to San Juan Hills, with open ground to the right in the direction of sugar house, with a slight ridge running from house to near the woods.

Finding vacant ground at lower part of the ridge, near woods, the Second Squadron, three troops, took position, there connecting with other troops on its right, and opened fire on the earthworks located between the block houses, and on the block house to the left of it, against which troops were advancing. For a time the enemy's fire was very heavy on our position, but our fire soon had effect; as the enemy's fire slackened, the squadron advanced without check to crest of San Juan Hills. Two of my troops, C and F, going to the right of a body of water in our front, and G troop through the left end of it with myself. The troop commander, Lieutenant Smith, as was Lieutenant Shipp, being killed at last position. C and F troops arrived on the hill to the right of the road, and G troop to the left of it at earthworks. I sent for C and F troops to join me on left of road, as there were no other troops at that point at that time, but before the order was complied with other troops of the regiment came up and my two troops were ordered to remain to right of road.

Captain Beck with his troop joined on my left, and Captain Ayres with his troop joined about twenty minutes later from the direction of the woods to our left and rear. (A few men of Troop D also came on line.) He reported his arrival to Colonel Wood and was placed on line to left of road; later I was ordered by Regimental Commander to take charge of troops on that part of line and open fire, which continued about ten minutes, when firing ceased and line was withdrawn behind crest of hill, at which time I was wounded, about 5:45 p. m., and taken to the rear.

During the action up to this time, the officers and men of the troops with me behaved in a manner to entitle them to the highest praise. Officers were cool and quick to carry out orders, and the men prompt and fearless in obeying. Captain Jones, Lieutenants Smith, Anderson, Roberts and Whitehead came specially under my notice and conducted themselves in a most satisfactory manner. Lieutenant Pershing, R. Q. M., was with the second squadron when posted on Sugar House Hill, and during its advance on San Juan Hills; he conducted himself in a most gallant and efficient manner.

I would like to mention several enlisted men of Troop G for their coolness and daring, but am not sufficiently acquainted with them to state their names positively and without reference to records. Among the number was the first sergeant, a trumpeter, I believe Whiteby name, two men who came to my assistance in dragging Lieutenant Smith from under fire after he was hit, and two men who dragged myself from under fire after being wounded. The first sergeant was very active and efficient in commanding troop after the death of Lieutenant Smith, and the trumpeter kept with me and was prompt in sounding calls, as ordered. By inquiry, no doubt, all these men can be identified and proper credit given them.

I remain, very respectfully,
(Signed) THEO. J. WINT,
Major Tenth Cavalry.

TROOP C, TENTH CAVALRY

In camp in front of Santiago de Cuba, July 5, 1898.

The Adjutant, Tenth Cavalry.

Sir: Pursuant to instructions, I have the honor to report the part taken by Troop C, Tenth Cavalry, in the engagement in front of Santiago on July 1 and 2, 1898:

The troop, with one officer and fifty-one men, left its camp (with the regiment) at 4:30 p. m., June 30, and bivouacked that night on the road about four hundred yards south of the sugar mill, and after the artillery engagement on July 1 left at 9:20 a. m. for the line of block houses held by the enemy.

About 10:30 a. m., while on the road, the enemy opened fire. Packs were dropped and left under guard, and the troop ordered into the river bottom, where it remained about half an hour, for protection from fire until it could deploy. While here a shell burst over the troop and I was struck by a small fragment in the left side above the point of the hip and received a slight flesh wound. My troop cut the wire fence to the right of the creek and deployed into the woods in rear of the front line of the regiment, and lay under cover in support on the right of the Second Squadron until the command to advance was given.

While advancing, and near the road, Colonel Wood, the brigade commander, came by and told me to move my troop to the right and toward the block house. I had one man killed and seven wounded in reaching the top of the hill. Captain Jones came up with Troop F, Tenth Cavalry, soon after I reached the block house, and I reported my troop to him and formed, with his, a skirmish line and moved on to the block house and entrenchments on the next hill. Here my troop got separated from Captain Jones's, but with eighteen men of my own and several from other organizations moved forward about four hundred yards when the fire became very severe and I had two men wounded, and halted.

After passing the entrenchments on the second hill my line joined that of Lieutenants Fleming and Miller of Troop I, Tenth Cavalry, which was on my right, and from then our line was continuous. Shortly, Colonel Roosevelt and part of his regiment joined our right and I reported to him with my troop. His command took position behind the crest which we now occupied, and that night my troop and Troop I entrenched and held the trenches during July 2 and 3 and joined the regiment July 4.

Casualties: Killed—One man. Wounded—One officer, nine men.

Very respectfully,
EDWARD D. ANDERSON,
First Lieutenant, Tenth Cavalry, Commanding Troop.

Before Santiago de Cuba, July 5, 1898.

The Adjutant, Tenth United States Cavalry.

Sir: In compliance with instructions from your office I have the honor to submit the following report concerning the part taken by Troop D, Tenth Cavalry, while in action against the Spaniards July 1, 2 and 3:

On the morning of July 1, Troop D, under command of Captain John Bigelow, Jr., occupied the line of outposts and performed this duty until withdrawn preparatory to the forward movement. While advancing along the road, and in close proximity to the balloon, the troop was subjected to a very severe artillery and small-arms fire, but remained orderly and unshaken. Sergeant Hatcher was wounded at this time. The fire becoming more severe, the troop was ordered to take cover, which they retained only a few minutes. The deployment was made to the left and occupied considerable time owing to the great difficulty met with in getting through the dense underbrush and chaparral. The line being formed, Troop D, occupying the extreme left, crossed creek and moved toward block house on left of road leading to Santiago. Two wire fences were met with, which, owing to the absence of wire nippers, held the troop unnecessarily long under a well-directed and deadly fire. At the first fence one private is believed to have been killed; at the second one was severely wounded. Beyond the fence the troop advanced under a heavy fire and charged the block house on the hill. When at a distance of about seventy-five yards from the block house, Captain Bigelow received three wounds and was removed to the rear by Privates Henderson and Boarman, Troop D. This removal took place under a heavy fire.

Corporal J. Walker was probably the first soldier to reach the top of the hill and is believed to have shot the Spaniard who killed Lieutenant Ord. The troop remained in the vicinity of the block house until ordered to join the regiment to the right of block house and were under fire, then under command of Major Wint. A portion of the troop under my command became separated during some turning movement, and as soon as I learned that contact with the troop was lost I moved on block house near ford. From this point I marched my detachment, under heavy fire, at a double time across field between two block houses, intending to connect with what appeared to be troops of the Tenth Cavalry, who were to my left and front. When part way across, I was halted by General Sumner and ordered to place my men in position and to act as a part of his reserve. On July 2 and 3 the troop took up position in the line of investment.

Very respectfully,
A. E. KENNINGTON,
Lieutenant, Tenth Cavalry, Commanding Troop D.

Camp A. G. Forse, Huntsville, Ala., December 19, 1898.
Adjutant General, U. S. A., Washington, D. C. (Through military channels).

Sir: I have the honor to submit the following report of the part taken by Troop D, Tenth Cavalry, in the engagements before Santiago de Cuba, so far as it is known to me:

On the 30th of June the troop marched with the second squadron of the Tenth Cavalry, Major Wint's, from Sevilla, and encamped a few hundred yards beyond El Poso on an eminence overlooking the basin of the San Juan river, or creek. My troop served as support to Lieutenant Smith's, which was on picket about one hundred yards to its front. In the morning it was placed on picket, relieving Lieutenant Smith's troop. Soon after my sentinels were posted I was ordered to withdraw my troop and prepare to march. Having done so, I took my place with my troop in the column and, after waiting half an hour to an hour for the column to move, marched with the column past El Poso and the division military hospital in the direction of San Juan. The military balloon passed over our regiment from rear to front while we were at a halt. At a halt made soon afterwards I was ordered to have my men strip themselves of everything but arms and ammunition. The rolls, haversacks, and canteens of my men were taken off and laid on the ground near the road and two men detailed to remain with them as guard. About this time our balloon commenced coming down near the head of our regiment. When about one hundred feet from the ground it was fired at by the enemy's artillery. About the same time we received a volley of infantry fire coming down the road over our heads too high to strike anyone. The troop ahead of mine started to the rear, but was soon checked. I understand that the impulse to break to the rear was imparted to it by the Seventy-first New York. My men were lying down in the road facing the left, by order of the squadron commander, Major Wint. The enemy's fire, delivered in volleys, kept raking the road and riddling the dense foliage about us. I thought that the enemy had the range of our position, or at least the direction of this road, and that the situation demanded that the troops be moved off the road either to the right or left, or formed so as to face in the direction from which the fire was coming. I looked around for the squadron commander to get his permission to move my troop off the road, or to make a change of front with it to the right. He was not anywhere in sight. I had seen him some time before going toward the right of our line, or head of our column. After waiting some time for him to return, I acted on my own responsibility by bringing my troop around at right angle to the road, its right resting on the road, its left lying in the wood. In this position I was free from the troop on my right, in case it should again break to the rear. I was under the impression that we were much nearer the enemy than afterwards proved to be the case, and expected the regiment to deploy across the road at any minute.

From my studying of tactics and the drill regulations, together with my limited experience in field exercises, I knew that in dismounted fighting, especially in a densely wooded country, the time comes when the direction of operations is necessarily left to the company commanders, and I judged that this time had come or could not be far off. I did not know but that the squadron commander was disabled, and I was determined that my men should not be decimated without doing any execution, through fear of responsibility or lack of initiative on my part. I felt that it would be erring on the right side to anticipate slightly the proper time for independent action on the part of company commanders. After waiting a minute or two in my new position, the enemy's fire not abating and no superior officer appearing, I faced my troop to the left and pushed into the wood far enough to clear the road by about ten or twenty yards with the rear of my column, when I came upon a line of infantry skirmishers apparently without officers. I had my troop face to the right, or in the general direction in which the road ran, and prepared to advance. In anticipation of the difficulty of penetrating the dense undergrowth I took immediate charge of one platoon and gave my lieutenant, Second Lieutenant A. E. Kennington, Tenth Cavalry, charge of the other, with instructions to keep his platoon in touch with mine. I then proceeded to advance in a direction generally parallel to the road which I had just left. I expected that by the time I arrived abreast of the head of my regiment I would find it deployed or deploying. Under the enemy's unaimed fire we pushed through the dense wood and undergrowth, waded a creek about knee deep, and a short distance beyond it came upon a line of troops lying in a road; but it was not our regiment. Here I received word from my lieutenant that he, with his platoon, was some distance to my right. He inquired whether he should join me. As there was a heavy fire coming down the road, and I did not wish to expose his men unnecessarily, I answered in the negative. The bearer of the message to and from me was Sergeant George Dyals, of my troop, who was afterwards wounded so that he lost the sight of one eye. He has since been discharged for physical disability.

The wood terminated in a thin belt just beyond this road. After lying a few minutes in the road I proceeded with my platoon through this belt of wood and came upon open ground overgrown with tall grass reaching nearly to the waist. Here the enemy's fire seemed to come principally from our left. I accordingly faced my men to the left, and filed off in that direction. As a number of bullets dropped near us, Sergeant John Elliott of my troop came up to me, and pointing to a tree on our right, said that he saw something stirring in it; that it looked like a Spaniard, and that he would like my permission to fire at it. I looked at the tree, but it was so dense that I could not see into it. I had been cautioned by troops whom I had passed against firing, as there were troops in front. Remarking that it might be a Cuban or one of our own men, I refused the permission.

Soon afterwards, while we were lying down, Private George Stovall of my troop was shot through the heart and killed; the same shot wounded Private Wade Bledsoe in the thigh. About one hundred yards farther on we came upon a squad of infantrymen sitting under some trees on the edge of the aforementioned belt of wood, around an officer who was lying on his back bleeding from the face, and who died while we were there. I believe that this officer and Privates Stovall and Bledsoe were shot by the sharpshooter whom Sergeant Elliott wanted to fire at. The infantrymen stated that our men were falling back and the Spaniards advancing. We could not see any enemy. On our left was a stream which I took to be the one we had crossed. From the other side of it came sounds of voices and loud reports of firing. We could not tell whether they were Spaniards or American, but I thought it was best to take our chances on their being American. We accordingly waded the stream, and pushing into the wood on the opposite bank, found ourselves among the men of General Hawkins' brigade. They were lying in a road on the edge of the wood. Beyond them stretched a plain about six hundred yards wide, overgrown with tall grass like that through which we had just passed. At the farther edge of the plain was a hill about 150 feet high, now known to our troops at San Juan Hill, or a part of it. On the top of this hill was a block house and a structure that looked like a shed. Here and there puffs of light smoke indicated that the position was manned by infantry firing at the enemy on the hill. It seemed to be falling back on the main line. There was no firing in the latter. My men and myself lay down in this road with the infantry. Everybody whom I could then see was lying down except one officer of infantry, who was walking up and down the road in the rear of the line exposed to a fire which raked the road. From conversation with officers of the Sixteenth Infantry I understand that this was Captain George H. Palmer of that regiment. I asked him whether it was not about time to advance to the support of the line out in the plain which seemed to me to be falling back. He replied that he supposed it would be pretty soon, and kept on walking as before.

Sergeant Elliott of my troop asked permission to go up to the fence and do some firing. I replied, "Go ahead, sergeant, if you think you can do any good." He accordingly stood up by the fence and fired seven shots, when, having attracted the enemy's fire, he fell back and lay down.

Immediately in front of us, beyond the road, ran a barbed wire fence. There were no wire nippers in my troop. With a view to an advance through this fence, I dug with my hands at one of the fence posts, but soon concluded that I could not accomplish anything in that way. I then stood up and pulled and pushed at the post, but made no appreciable impression on it. So I lay down again and continued looking out on the plain for signs of an advance. After a while I observed near the edge of the open plain on our left a swarm of men breaking forward from the road. I went up to the top of the wire fence by stepping from wire to wire near a post, and jumped off the top, calling to my men as I struck the ground to come on. Corporal John Walker of my troop got a bayonet and cut the wire. My men and a number of infantrymen went through the opening thus made. I struck out as fast as the tall grass would permit me toward the common objective of the mass of men which I now saw surging forward on my right and left—San Juan Hill. The men kept up a steady double time, and commenced firing of their own accord over one another's heads and the heads of the officers, who were well out in front of the men. I tried to stop the firing, as I thought it would seriously retard the advance, and the officers near me tried to do it; but a constant stream of bullets went over our heads, the men halting in an erect position to fire. The men covered, I should say, about fifty yards from front to rear. They formed a swarm rather than a line. When they were not firing they seemed to be all cheering and yelling. Our firing, though wild, was not altogether ineffective, and retarded the advance less than I had thought it would. I could see the side of the hill dotted with little clouds of dust thrown up by our bullets. We evidently peppered it pretty hotly from top to bottom, and I learned since then that many dead and wounded Spaniards were found in the trenches on top of the hill. These casualties, however, were caused in part, perhaps mostly, by the fire of our small advance line prior to the assault. This line was composed, I understand, mostly of classified marksmen and sharpshooters.

As we approached the foot of the hill our artillery commenced firing over our heads at the enemy on top of it. This caused a slowing up in the general advance. When I was about half way up the hill I was disabled by three bullet wounds received simultaneously.

I had already received one, but did not know it. What took place subsequent to my disablement, in the direction of the enemy, is known to me only through the statements of my men and others, substantiated by the depositions inclosed herewith. My platoon went to the top of the hill with the infantry, and was soon afterwards conducted by Lieutenant J. J. Pershing, regimental quartermaster, Tenth Cavalry, to the line of the Tenth Cavalry, a short distance to the right.

The following men of the platoon especially distinguished themselves: Sergeant James Elliott, Corporal John Walker, and Private (now Corporal) Luchious Smith. Sergeant Elliott and Private Smith were, during the ascent of the hill, constantly among the bolder few who voluntarily made themselves ground scouts, drawing the attention of the enemy from the main line upon themselves. Corporal Walker was with the handful of fearless spirits who accompanied Lieutenant Ord, one of the Sixth United States Infantry, forming with that splendid young soldier the point of General Hawkins's gallant brigade, the head

MAJ. GEN. WILLARD A. HOLBROOK
CHIEF OF CAVALRY

and front of the assault; and it was Corporal Walker who avenged the death of Lieutenant Ord.

First Sergeant William H. Givens was with the platoon which I commanded. Whenever I observed him he was at his post exercising a steadying or encouraging influence upon the men, and conducting himself like the thorough soldier which I have long known him to be. I understand, to my great satisfaction, that he has been rewarded by an appointment to a lieutenancy in an immune regiment.

I think it due to the other men of my troop to say that, with one exception, they proved themselves ready to follow me wherever I would lead them. Their conduct made me prouder than ever of being an officer in the American Army, and of wearing the insignia of the Tenth United States Cavalry.

The movements of the platoon commanded by Lieutenant Kennington have, I believe, been reported to you by that officer.

I took into action, including Lieutenant Kennington's platoon, but not including the two men left to guard the packs, two officers and 48 men. My losses were as follows:

Killed—Private George Stovall. Wounded—Captain John Bigelow, Jr., Sergeant George Dyals, Sergeant Willis Hatcher, Private J. H. Campbell, Private Henry Fearn, Private Fred Shockley, Private Harry Sturgis, and Private James F. Taylor. Missing—Private James Clay.

The accompanying map, marked D, is intended to show roughly the course taken by my troop after it left the regiment, and the general direction of the attack made by the regiment.

Very respectfully,
JOHN BIGELOW, JR.,
Captain, Tenth Cavalry, Commanding Troop D.

Near Santiago, Cuba, July 5, 1898.

Adjutant Tenth Cavalry.

Sir: I have the honor to submit the following report of the action which took place on this field July 1, 2 and 3, 1898:

Troop F, Tenth Cavalry, which I commanded, was in column of twos in the road at a halt awaiting the passage of a column of infantry when fire from the Spanish entrenchments opened. The troop came under a very dense fire—musketry and artillery—at once, with no means of determining from whence the fire came, as all view was entirely cut off by the densest underbrush which lined the road, and no effective cover to get to. After something like half an hour of this fire the squadron was put in the attacking line as support and moved forward. In the brush and amid the roar of guns all sight of the firing line and touch of adjoining troops was lost. Lieutenant Whitehead, with a part of the second platoon, were also separated from the troop, and I think passed in front of the troop from left to right during the advance. Lieutenant Whitehead joined his detachment to the first command he met and advanced with it. The troop advanced at double time on the enemy's works as soon as out of the brush and in sight of the works. On arriving on the hill on which the works stood it was found that the works were carried and the Spaniards were retreated to the next crest. The troops had become mixed up in a crowd of disorganized soldiers at the works. It was at once assembled, line of skirmish was formed, the advance taken up in the direction of the retreat of the enemy. While at the first works Lieutenant Anderson, with a part of Troop C, reported to me as the senior officer of the regiment present and was put on the skirmish line on the right of my troops. We advanced together over the next ridge and down it to within about five hundred yards of the works at present occupied by the enemy. Here we remained for some time exchanging fire with the enemy in the works. My left was on the road. There were troops on my left, and a little less advanced, and troops on my right a little more advanced, but their firing was not strong. Being, so far as I know, unsupported, I sent word back to the squadron commander describing my position, and was ordered to return to the crest of the hill which our troops now occupy on the road. Here I received word that the hill was to be held at all hazards. The troop occupied the crest, exchanging fire with the enemy, until dark. During the night a trench was dug and occupied at daylight, the morning of the 2nd. The troop remained in this trench until late in the afternoon, every exposure at the trench drawing fire from the enemy. The fire was returned only when several of the enemy exposed themselves at once. On the night of the 2nd the troop was joined with the regiment and moved farther to the right on the general line, where it was again entrenched, and has remained in the trenches to the present time.

Lieutenant Whitehead, who was separated from the troop at the commencement of the advance, returned to it soon after it reached its most advanced position, bringing his detachment with him.

I wish to mention both Lieutenant Anderson, who was with me from the termination of the first assault, and Lieutenant Whitehead for their coolness and bravery. I could only do justice to the troop by mentioning by name all who were engaged, not only for their bravery, but for their splendid discipline under the most demoralizing fire.

Killed—First Lieutenant W. E. Shipp, on temporary staff duty. Wounded—Second Lieutenant H. C. Whitehead, slightly, and continued in action; Sergeant Amos Elliston, Sergeant Frank Rankin, Corporal Allen Jones, Blacksmith Charles Robertson, Private Ison Taylor, Private Benjamin West.

Very respectfully,
T. W. JONES,
Captain, Tenth Cavalry, Commanding Troop F.

Report of Gun Detachment, Second Cavalry Brigade, composed of Tenth Cavalry, on July 1:

Before Santiago de Cuba, July 1, 1898.

Adjutant General Second Cavalry Brigade.

Sir: I have the honor to report that on July 1, 1898, this detachment went into action on the road about one hundred yards beyond the first crossing of the San Juan Creek and opened up on the block house and entrenchment about six hundred yards to the right of the road and did some effective work with eight or ten shots, and, not having any cover, was forced to retire, having two men wounded in a very few minutes—Sergeant J. G. L. Taylor, Troop E, Tenth Cavalry, and Private Peter Saunders, Troop B, Tenth Cavalry. I later opened fire with one gun on hill at second block house nearest town, on an entrenchment occupied by Spanish troops, and forced them to leave the same. After a few shots I was relieved by a light battery and retired. Shortly after, with two Hotchkiss guns and a machine gun, I took position on crest occupied by a troop of the First United States Cavalry, (Captain Galbraith's), and with the Hotchkiss guns did some effective work on a blockhouse in our immediate front, about eight hundred or nine hundred yards distant. The machine gun did good work on an entrenchment.

I wish to mention as particularly meritorious and gallant, Sergeant Watson and Private Saunders, both of Troop B, Tenth Cavalry, in aiding a wounded corporal of the Third Cavalry to a hospital under a heavy artillery fire, he being deserted by everyone else. The same men deserve special mention for their magnificent behavior during the entire time they were in action. Private Saunders was wounded in the first action and taken to the rear. I also want to mention Private Daniels of Troop F for gallant behavior in the first action.

Very respectfully,
JAMES B. HUGHES,
First Lieutenant, Tenth Cavalry, Commanding Detachment.

TROOP G, TENTH CAVALRY

Camp Albert G. Forse, Ala., November 30th, 1898.

The Adjutant General, Fourth Army Corps.

Sir: In compliance with request of Major General Wheeler, I have the honor to submit the following report of the action of this troop from the morning of July 1st until 1 p. m. of the same day.

The troop was drawn in from outpost duty about 6:30 a. m. July 1st, and about 9 a. m. moved from El Poso down the road toward the Spanish position. While in the road they were passed by a balloon, which shortly afterward drew a heavy fire from the Spanish.

A short distance from the point where the road crosses the river we were halted and ordered to lie down, and remained in that place until orders were brought to move to the right into the bed of the river. This we accomplished with some delay owing to a strong fence of barbed wire through the undergrowth along the river.

After reforming in the river bed we moved up stream a few hundred yards and took such shelter as was afforded by the river bank. The fire at this time was very heavy, projectiles from both artillery and small arms falling around and among the troops.

At about 12:30 p. m. the troop moved up the bed of a small creek that flowed in from our right, and by direction of Major Wint came into an open space in sight of and facing what I have since heard called the Sugar House Ridge. Here the troop was deployed and just as the first advance was ordered I received a wound through the body that prevented my advancing with the troop. When I last saw them they were advancing in good order at the double time toward the two block houses in our front.

The conduct of the men was good and I saw no inclination to hesitate or to straggle.

I desire to especially mention the conduct of Private William J. Davis and Trumpeter James Cooper of this troop, who assisted me from the spot where I fell back to the river under a very sharp fire and rendered much assistance in trying circumstances both to myself and to Acting Assistant Surgeon Delgado, into whose hospital I was taken and which had to be broken up on account of its becoming too much exposed to the enemy's fire. The conduct of these two men, in my opinion, entitles them to the medal of honor for rescuing wounded at the risk of their own lives.

Referring to the report of Major T. J. Wint, Tenth Cavalry, I have the honor to state that the trumpeter of Troop G, to whom he refers, is Trumpeter Zachariah Steward, whose conduct I have heard highly spoken of.

I regret that I am not able to give a more complete and definite account of this action, but I did not get far enough before being wounded to get a very clear idea of our position with reference to other troops or to the Spanish works.

Very respectfully,
T. A. ROBERTS,
Second Lieutenant, Tenth U. S. Cavalry, Commanding Troop G.

APPENDIX "E"

COMMENDATORY LETTER BY MAJOR GENERAL JOE WHEELER.

Headquarters Cavalry Division, Camp Wikoff, L. I., September 20, 1898.
To the Officers and Soldiers of the Cavalry Division, Army of Santiago:

The duties for which the troops comprising the Cavalry Division were brought together have been accomplished.

On June 14th we sailed from Tampa, Florida, to encounter in the sickly season the diseases of the tropical island of Cuba, and to face and attack the historic legions of Spain in positions chosen by them and which for years they had been strengthening by every art and contrivance known to the skillful military engineers of Europe.

On the 23rd, one squadron each of the First and Tenth Regular Cavalry and two squadrons of the First Volunteer Cavalry, in all 964 officers and men, landed on Cuban soil. These troops marched on foot fourteen miles, and, early on the morning of the 24th, attacked and defeated double their number of regular Spanish soldiers under the command of Lieutenant General Linares. Eagerly and cheerfully you pushed onward, and on July 1st the First, Third, Sixth, Ninth and Tenth Cavalry and the First Volunteer Cavalry, forded the San Juan River and gallantly swept over San Juan Hill, driving the enemy from its crest. Without a moment's halt you formed, aligning the division upon the First Infantry Division under General Kent, and, together with these troops, you bravely charged and carried the formidable entrenchments of Fort San Juan. The entire force which fought and won this great victory was less than seven thousand men.

The astonished enemy, though still protected by the strong works to which he had made his retreat, was so stunned by your determined valor that his only thought was to devise the quickest means of saving himself from further battle. The great Spanish fleet hastily sought escape from the harbor and was destroyed by our matchless Navy.

After seizing the fortifications of San Juan Ridge you, in the darkness of night, strongly entrenched the position your valor had won. Reinforced by Bates' Brigade on your left and Lawton's Division on your right, you continued the combat until the Spanish Army of

Santiago Province succumbed to the superb prowess and courage of American arms. Peace promptly followed, and you return to receive the plaudits of seventy millions of people.

The valor displayed by you was not without sacrifice. Eighteen per cent, or nearly one in five, of the Cavalry Division fell on the field either killed or wounded. We mourn the loss of these heroic dead, and a grateful country will always revere your memory.

Whatever may be my fate, wherever my steps may lead, my heart will always burn with increasing admiration for your courage in action, your fortitude under privation and your contant devotion to duty in its highest sense, whether in battle, in bivouac or upon the march.

JOE WHEELER,
Major General, U. S. V., Commanding.

APPENDIX "F"

Camp at Casas Grandes, Mexico, March 19, 1916.

Colonel W. C. Brown, Tenth U. S. Cavalry.

Sir: Information has been received that Villa bandits, consisting of about two hundred men, are in the vicinity of San Miguel, where they are probably gathering horses and supplies. You will entrain two squadrons of your regiment at once and proceed south, disembarking one squadron at Cuevitas, sending the other squadron, under Major Evans, to disembark at Las Varas.

You will proceed with the squadron which disembarks at Cuevitas to the edge of the woods surrounding the San Miguel plains on the Cuevitas trail. From this point you will proceed to the San Miguel Ranch so as to reach there just before dawn March 20, 1916. You will destroy or capture any forces or supplies of Villa that may be found there. In case of flight you will follow bandits, sending information of direction taken to the columns under Major Evans and Colonel Erwin.

Colonel Erwin with the Seventh Cavalry will reach a point west of El Valle tonight to cooperate with your column. He will advance on San Miguel via the Cerrillo Canyon and reach the edge of the San Miguel plain at daylight March 20th, there await the result of your attack, ready to act as circumstances may require.

Major Evans on disembarking at Las Veras will remain there to close the trail leading southwest from San Miguel.

In case of pursuit the commanders of all columns will cooperate to accomplish this mission.

By command of General Pershing.

J. A. RYAN,
Major Thirteenth Cavalry, Acting Chief of Staff.

APPENDIX "G"

From: W. C. Brown, Tenth Cavalry, at Cusi, April 5, '16, noon.
To: General Pershing by aeroplane.

April 1st having received no reply from message sent to Colonel Dodd March 30th, and having sent to the R. R., San Antonio, to communicate with division headquarters, left Major Evans April 1st at San Juan del Monte to guard that pass and road, and proceeded with Young's squadron on road to Guerrero expecting to meet Colonel Dodd there.

About twelve miles out, at a place called Aguas Calientes, where there are four or five ranches, we were fired on by Mexicans who, it was later found, was Beltran's band of about one hundred and fifty (estimated roughly), of Villistas. After a few minutes' firing they retreated over a rough wooded ridge to our left. Major Young sent Troops H and F to attack them in flank, which proved a good move. The enemy made a precipitate retreat at once. Killed three; so reported by escaped Carranza prisoners, who saw them shot. We saw but two. No casualties on our side except an F Troop horse, which died on 3rd.

The enemy left the pack outfit of a machine gun, and we learned next day that they still had one machine gun which was out of order. The running fight conducted mainly by H and F Troops in wooded mountains to southeast of Aguas Calientes and the command assembled after dark at small ranch called El Mestina.

April 2nd I took the southermost and largest trail, with H and G Troops and two machine guns; Major Young, E and F, and two machine guns. Young soon lost his smaller trail and camped at Napa Veche Ranch on edge of Bostill's plain. I followed my trail for six or seven miles when it seemed to go out on the plain where tracks scattered and trail was lost. Its general direction was east by south and over mountains so exceedingly rough and rocky that it was barely passable by leading the mounts. I camped that night at Napa Veche.

As we left camp (two miles out) two natives approached and said that they were Carrancistas who had been impressed by Villa. Said Beltran was short of ammunition. We sent to their camp and got four rifles, three mules and one pony, and two more men, one of whom is thought to be a Villista and is sent back with the pack train. The others were, on the 3rd inst., released at the suggestion of one of the Carranza officers with us.

April 3rd marched thirteen miles to San Antonio. We followed the trail the most of the way but it soon diminished to a few tracks. I am now of the opinion that the main trail went nearly due south of Napa Veche and crossed the R. R. some five to eight miles west of San Antonio.

A Mr. Locke, an American hotel keeper of Minaca, came into our camp and told of the attack at Minaca at 4 a. m. some days previous. Two of his companions were killed but he escaped.

N. B.—Late April 1st I sent two native guides (pacificos) on two of our mules to Major Evans, advising him of our fight and to look out for enemy debouching on the big plain. Have not heard whether he got the message. Sent another to him from Napa Veche April 2nd. Same result.

Guides and messengers are hard to get as they fear retaliation by Villa for serving the Americans. To send a message on night of 1st inst. to me had to deposit his watch and diamond ring as security for return of messenger. At San Antonio we found it impossible to send telegrams unless prepaid, though urgency of matter was represented. I sold a $2.50 knife to a soldier for fifty cents to get money to send one short official telegram. This condition has become so intolerable that at Cusi today I found I could get Mexican coin and checks on my personal check.

I have drawn my personal check today for $1,100.00 gold to loan to officers and the quartermaster to purchase supplies, forage and rations. I had previously spent my last cent for this purpose and drawn personal checks for $160.00 for same purpose.

Since leaving the railroad on 20th we have had hay or fodder three times, and about one-third of the allowance each time. Have lost about four or five horses from corn colic.

We have practically no horseshoes left, and from now on shoes lost will leave horses unshod. Men have lived on fresh beef, tortillas made from corn meal which we have ground ourselves, and in the main in good health. We left one man sick at San Antonio this morning. We have men afoot, but for fact that I got six Villa mounts at La Temada, bought several and captured several. I think I can go another week and am marching on S. Boria where I expect to get in touch again with Carranza troops and put this squadron and machine gun troop where it will be most effective. My personal opinion is, however, that the various demoralized Villa bands will soon (if not now) be so scattered that it will prove fruitless to follow them.

One F trooper, who was walking on punishment given by Captain Valentine for disobedience of orders, deserted April 1. I understand Major Tompkins' command saw him at a ranch.

Don't know where Evans is, but he is enterprising and I am satisfied that if he got my message of the 1st he is doing all possible.

We should have a wireless outfit for each squadron. Captain Foulois has given me a map much needed, and Lieutenant Deuel is mapping the country as we go along.

W. C. BROWN,

Colonel, Tenth Cavalry.

APPENDIX "H"

Camp at San Geronimo, April 5, 1916.

Colonel W. C. Brown,
    Tenth Cavalry,
        Enroute South from Cusi.

Sir:

1. Colonel Dodd, with Seventh Cavalry, is near Santa Tomas. Major Evans arrived at Namiquipa today. Major Howze is near Guerrero and moving southeast toward San Borja. Lieutenant Colonel Allen, Eleventh Cavalry, leaves here tomorrow for San Antonio and points south.

2. From all information received it is believed that Villa, with an escort, is going to Parral, being carried in a stretcher or carriage.

The Commanding General directs that in order to cut Villa off that you proceed from Cusi to Parral via Bananoleva, Satevo, Valle de Zargosa-Sapien. You are reminded that Colonel Cano has moved in that direction and from him guides may be procured who will be of great assistance.

Your movement may also shield movements of Major Tompkins and Major Howze, who are following Villa's trail.

3. On arrival at Parral you will be guided by the information you secure.

4. An advance sub-base will be established at San Antonio, on the railroad, from which a pack train will be sent you carrying horseshoes, nails, salt, money, and other supplies.

5. Exhausted men and worn out animals will be sent to San Antonio where they will be cared for until fit for service.

6. Every effort possible should be made to reach Parral without delay.

7. It is not understood why you have not been able to send reports of your column, and the Commanding General directs that his orders on this subject be strictly complied with.

8. You are authorized to employ guides, interpreters, secret service men, or other individuals who may be of service to you, and to purchase all kinds of supplies that you may need. Money will be furnished you from here and an effort will also be made to send you money through the American Consul at Chihuahua.

9. You will make every effort to cooperate with our own columns and those of the Carranza forces operating in your vicinity with a view to accomplish the object of your mission.

10. Send reports to San Antonio.

                J. A. RYAN,
     Major, Thirteenth Cavalry, I. O. Acting Chief of Staff.

APPENDIX "I"

From: Colonel W. C. Brown, Tenth Cavalry, Santa Cruz, April 12th, 8 p. m.

To: General Pershing.

Subject: Engagement of Major Tompkins' command with Carranza troops at Parral April 12.

I desire to report that while in camp near Sapien about 6:30 p. m., three Thirteenth Cavalrymen of Major Tompkins' Squadron came to our camp with word that the squadron had been attacked by Carrancistas in Parral and had retreated to this place where they had made a stand and that several men had been killed and that fighting was going on when they left the command. Leaving our two pack mules and led horses with a small guard at the little ranch where we were camped, we were in saddle in ten minutes and reached this place, eight miles south, in one hour; arriving after dark and some two hours after the Carranza forces had ceased firing.

I found Tompkins' squadron here, where the ranch buildings afforded a fine defensive position. Tompkins and Lieutenant Ord were slightly wounded, the former in the left breast and the latter in the left ear. Four (4) troopers were wounded, and Sergeant Ridgley, Troop M, Thirteenth Cavalry, and Private Ledford, Troom M, Thirteenth Cavalry, killed. The names of the wounded are Corporal McGee, Troop M, shot in mouth; Corporal Willingham, Troop K, leg; Corporal Tannous, Troop K, right forearm; Private Schonburger, slight wound in left hip; Private Eichenberger, Troop M, with rear guard, is missing.

From Major Tompkins and his officers the following particulars of the fight and events leading up to it were gathered:

When Major Tompkins camped at Valle de Zaragosa (Concho) General Lozano, of the Carrancista forces at Parral, sent a captain and lieutenant to Concho where they arrived late at night for consultation with Major Tompkins. They appeared to be very much pleased with the appearance of American troops in this district, a fact that I noticed on the part of people generally when I arrived twenty-four hours later.

These officers announced that they were subject to Major Tompkins' orders. The captain stated that Tompkins would be well received in Parral and that he (Tompkins) should reach Parral about 11 a. m. April 12th. The march was planned accordingly and the command arrived at the designated time.

He entered the town with the advance guard as an escort, proceeded to General Lozano's house where a conference was held. No new information of Villa could be obtained other than that he was not south of Parral. The General then said he would conduct Tompkins to a camping place, which he did, riding at the head of the column. As the rear of the column was leaving the outskirts of town for the camp it was fired upon by persons in the town.

This was reported to the General, and he at once returned to town to prevent further firing. Shortly after his departure a man in civilian dress, who seemed to be an official, came to Tompkins and begged him to withdraw in order to avoid a conflict. Tompkins explained at some length that his mission in Mexico was a peacable one and that he would do all in his power to prevent a conflict with Carranza troops, and as soon as the supplies, which had been ordered of one of the American merchants, arrived he (Tompkins) would march north. This man returned to a hill occupied by Mexican troops about seven hundred yards distant and held a conference with some of these troops, which immediately began to change their position to Tompkins' left flank. This move was checked by placing men on a more commanding position on our left.

The Carrancistas at once began firing from the front and left flank, and advancing at the same time from those directions. As a matter of self-preservation Tompkins was forced to return this fire, using but sixteen (16) men for this purpose, while the pack train and balance of the command withdrew to the north. The fire of the Mexicans was well aimed and heavy. They killed Sergeant Ridgely, and wounded Private Ledford in the left lung. The squadron withdrew slowly and in good order, finally reaching the main road, proceeding north to this place, Sta Cruz.

The pursuit was at first feeble and timid but gradually grew bolder as the numbers of the pursuers increased, which eventually was estimated at three hundred men. When about eight miles out of Parral the pursuit was so persistent that Tompkins took the rear guard of eight men and made a stand behind a stone wall, checking the pursuit and enabling the main body to get well clear of the pursuers. It was at this place that Tompkins and Ord were wounded and Private Chas. Eichenberg, Troop M, was missing, and three horses badly wounded. Another stand by the whole command was made four miles further on, and again, with half of Troop M, about one mile south of Sta Cruz.

This last stand appeared to be a surprise to the enemy and it is thought that ten or more were killed. The village of Sta Cruz was entered quietly and prepared for defense. The roofs of the buildings were manned by riflemen and the enemy kept at 1200 yards range. At 7:55 I arrived with Major Young's Squadron and the Machine Gun Troop. Tenth Cavalry, and assumed command. The enemy was still on the hill to the south when we arrived, as was shown by the sounding of their bugles after ours had been sounded.

For exceptional bravery in returning for a wounded man (Ledford) under a hot fire, Major Tompkins will recommend Lieutenant Ord for a Medal of Honor. This while Ord himself was wounded.

W. C. BROWN.

APPENDIX "J"

Colonel W. C. Brown, Tenth U. S. Cavalry.
Sir: News of the unprovoked assault upon your men in the town of Parral has just reached me at Satevo through Chihuahua. Ascertain if possible whether attack was directed by the local military commander of the de facto government, demanding of him a disavowal of this base act. If the attack was directed by the local civil authorities demand the immediate arrest of the responsible parties.

I am sending Lieutenant Colonel Allen with two troops to reinforce you. He should reach you tomorrow morning. Send word if possible to the columns under Major Tompkins and Major Howze of your situation.

Unless a satisfactory understanding has been reached by the time this message arrives, send word to Major Tompkins and Major Howze to join you at once. Place your command in a position of security and assume the defensive only so far as it is necessary to insure your safety.

The supply question may now become a serious one and you will be expected to meet your needs from the country round about.

Supplies will be sent you as soon as possible. Confer fully and confidentially with Captain Reed, who commands the escort bearing this message.

PERSHING.

Official:
J. A. RYAN,
Major, Thirteenth Cavalry I. O., Acting Chief of Staff.

APPENDIX "K"

The following letter from the citizens of Winooski, Vermont, serves to tell of the respect gained by the regiment during its tour of duty at Fort Ethan Allen, Vermont:

Winooski, Vt., June 29, 1916.
To General Funston, Commanding U. S. Army in Mexico:

As neighbors of Fort Ethan Allen, we, citizens of Winooski, Vermont, have a peculiar and personal interest in the welfare of the officers and men of the Tenth Regiment of U. S. Cavalry, who were stationed at this post for four years.

It was, therefore, with the deepest emotion that we read the dispatches telling of the treacherous ambush and attack on two troops of this gallant regiment by the Mexicans of Carranza's army at Carrizal in northern Mexico, in which Captain Boyd and Lieutenant Adair and a large number of their men were slain and Captain Morey desperately wounded and twenty or more men taken prisoners.

The valor displayed by officers and men in the face of almost certain death is in keeping with American traditions and unsurpassed in the annals of heroic deeds of all ages.

At a mass meeting of the citizens of Winooski, Vermont, held June 27th, 1916, and called to give recognition and support to the men who have responded to the call of the President, especially Company G of the Vermont National Guard, whose headquarters are at Winooski, and who left for the frontier on that day, speeches were made referring feelingly to these gallant officers and men of the Tenth U. S. Cavalry who so heroically met the treacherous attack of the Mexicans and shed the first American blood in the impending war between this country and the recognized government of Mexico.

A committee of seven were appointed to convey to the regiment through General Funston the deep and poignant grief of our citizens at the loss of these brave defenders, our pride because of their unsurpassed heroism and our appreciation of their undaunted courage and unexcelled patriotism displayed in such glorious deeds.

Therefore, through you to the commander of the Tenth U. S. Cavalry we express the sympathy, gratitude and appreciation of all of the citizens of this community because of these achievements of men who were our neighbors and friends and who met this supreme test and sacrifice in a manner to thrill and inspire every true American.

CHARLES S. LORD, Chairman.
JAMES TIMMONS, Pres. Village.
H. A. BAILEY, Ex-Pres. Village.
C. C. KELLOGG, C. Vt. Ry.
REV. R. H. WASHBURNE.
HENRY COULIN, Judge.
JOHN BEN GARY.

APPENDIX "L"

ROSTER OF REGIMENTAL OFFICERS, START OF PUNITIVE EXPEDITION

Field and Staff:
  Colonel W. C. Brown, Commanding.
  Major E. W. Evans, First Squadron.
  Major Charles Young, Second Squadron.
  Captain W. H. McCornick, Regimental Quartermaster.
  1st Lieut. H. R. Adair, Acting Adjutant.
  Captain John R. Barber, M. C., Surgeon.
  Captain C. C. Demmer, M. C., Asst. Surgeon.
  Veterinarian C. D. McMurdo.

Non-Commissioned Staff:
  Regimental Quartermaster Sergeant Hugh C. Scott.
  Squadron Sergeant Major James F. Booker.
  Squadron Sergeant Major William F. Scott.
  Sergeant James T. Penney, Troop C, Acting Color Sergeant.
  Corporal Will Green, Troop C, Acting Color Sergeant.

Troop A—1st Lieutenant Emmet Addis, Commanding Troop.
  2nd Lieutenant Eustis L. Hubbard.
  1st Sergeant Walter R. Sanders.

Troop B—Captain William C. Gardenhire, Commanding Troop.
  2nd Lieutenant Norman J. Boots.
  1st Sergeant Samuel H. Alexander.

Troop C—Captain George B. Pritchard, Commanding Troop.
  2nd Lieutenant Benjamin F. Hoge.
  1st Sergeant William Winrow.

Troop D—Captain Alfred E. Kennington, Commanding Troop.
  1st Lieutenant Reynold F. Migdalski.
  2nd Lieutenant Andrew L. Walton.
  1st Sergeant Reuben Horner.

Troop E—1st Lieutenant Selwyn D. Smith, Commanding Troop.
  2nd Lieutenant Henry Abbey, Jr.
  1st Sergeant (Acting) Buck Lane.

Troop F—Captain Wm. S. Valentine, Commanding Troop.
  2nd Lieutenant John Kennard.
  1st Sergeant James Allen.

Troop G—Captain George B. Rodney, Commanding Troop.
  2nd Lieutenant Thorne Deuel, Jr.
  1st Sergeant Andrew J. Hale.

Troop H—Captain Charles T. Boyd, Commanding Troop.
  1st Lieutenant Orlando C. Troxel.
  2nd Lieutenant Joseph F. Richmond.
  1st Sergeant Clifford A. Sandridge.

Troop I—Captain William L. Luhn, Commanding Troop.
  2nd Lieutenant Ray W. Barker.
  1st Sergeant Charles Dade.

Troop K—1st Lieutenant Albert B. Dockery, Commanding Troop.
  1st Sergeant Allan Peterson.

M. G. Troop—Captain Albert E. Phillips, Commanding Troop.
  1st Sergeant John H. Pappy.

Pursuant to telegraphic instructions from Commanding General, Punitive Expedition, March 14, 1916, Troop M, entrained at Nogales, Arizona, and proceeded by rail to Columbus, N. M., arriving March 16, 1916, and entered Mexico same date.

Troop M—1st Lieutenant Henry A. Meyer, Commanding Troop.
  2nd Lieutenant William B. Peebles.
  1st Sergeant Alonzo J. Day.

Pursuant to telegraphic instructions from Department Commander April 19, 1916,

Troop L left Fort Apache, Arizona, April 21, 1916, and reported to Commanding General, Punitive Expedition, at Columbus, N. M., April 24, 1916. Entered Mexico April 28, 1916.
Troop L—Captain Oliver P. M. Hazzard, Commanding Troop.
    1st Lieutenant Robert Blaine.
    1st Sergeant Charles H. Key.

APPENDIX "M"

ENLISTED MEN OF THE TENTH CAVALRY COMMISSIONED AS OFFICERS FROM THE DES MOINES TRAINING CAMP, OCTOBER 15, 1917.

Sergeant Miles M. Green, M. G. Troop, 10th Cavalry............Captain
Sergeant William Gillum, M. G. Troop, 10th Cavalry............Captain
1st Sgt. James Cranson, Troop E, 10th Cavalry............Captain
Reg. Q. M. Sgt. William W. Thompson, 10th Cavalry............Captain
1st Sgt. Walter R. Sanders, Troop A, 10th Cavalry............Captain
1st Sgt. Henry Houston, Troop K, 10th Cavalry............Captain
1st Sgt. William D. Peeks, Troop D, 10th Cavalry............Captain
Sergeant Howard D. Queen, Troop K, 10th Cavalry............Captain
Sergeant Edgar O. Malone, Troop F, 10th Cavalry............Captain
Q. M. Sgt. Fletcher Sewell, Troop A, 10th Cavalry............Captain
Sergeant Vance H. Marchbanks, Troop C, 10th Cavalry............Captain
1st Sgt. Clifford A. Sandridge, Troop H, 10th Cavalry............Captain
Sergeant Reuben Horner, Hq. Troop, 10th Cavalry............Captain
1st Sgt. Daniel Smith, Troop C, 10th Cavalry............Captain
Sq. Sgt. Major James F. Booker, 10th Cavalry............Captain
Sq. Sgt. Major William F. Scott, 10th Cavalry............Captain
Sergeant Hanson Johnson, Supply Troop, 10th Cavalry............Captain
Sergeant George C. Hall, Troop L, 10th Cavalry............Captain
Sq. Sgt. Major Edward W. Spearman, 10th Cavalry............Captain
Reg. Q. M. Sgt. William H. Williams, 10th Cavalry............Captain
Sergeant Robert T. Shobe, Troop C, 10th Cavalry............1st Lieutenant
Sergeant James E. Beard, M. G. Troop, 10th Cavalry............1st Lieutenant
Sergeant John Combs, Troop L, 10th Cavalry............1st Lieutenant
Sergeant Richard M. Norris, Troop A, 10th Cavalry............1st Lieutenant
Sergeant William T. Johnson, Troop A, 10th Cavalry............1st Lieutenant
Sergeant John Q. Lindsey, Hq. Troop, 10th Cavalry............1st Lieutenant
Sergeant John P. Walker, Troop E, 10th Cavalry............1st Lieutenant
Sergeant Floyd Gilmer, Troop A, 10th Cavalry............1st Lieutenant
Corporal Waddell C. Steele, Troop E, 10th Cavalry............1st Lieutenant
Sergeant Carey McLane, Troop L, 10th Cavalry............1st Lieutenant
Sergeant Walter Lyons, Troop C, 10th Cavalry............1st Lieutenant
Corporal William H. Brown, Jr., Troop D, 10th Cavalry............1st Lieutenant
Sergeant Hazel L. Raine, Troop F, 10th Cavalry............1st Lieutenant
Sergeant Rosen T. Brown, Troop D, 10th Cavalry............1st Lieutenant
Sergeant Russell Smith, Troop B, 10th Cavalry............1st Lieutenant
Sergeant Frank M. Goodner, Troop M, 10th Cavalry............1st Lieutenant
Sergeant Cleveland Morrow, Troop B, 10th Cavalry............1st Lieutenant
Sergeant Gus Williams, Troop D, 10th Cavalry............1st Lieutenant
Sergeant Vest Douglas, M. G. Troop, 10th Cavalry............1st Lieutenant
Sergeant Almando Henderson, Troop K, 10th Cavalry............1st Lieutenant
Sergeant George E. Edwards, Troop H, 10th Cavalry............1st Lieutenant
Sergeant William A. Stith, Troop M, 10th Cavalry............1st Lieutenant
Corporal William T. Burns, Troop D, 10th Cavalry............1st Lieutenant
Sergeant Stephen B. Barrow, Troop B, 10th Cavalry............2nd Lieutenant
Sergeant Clyde Roberts, Troop G, 10th Cavalry............2nd Lieutenant
Sergeant Benjamin Bettis, Troop A, 10th Cavalry............2nd Lieutenant
Sergeant William Collier, Troop B, 10th Cavalry............2nd Lieutenant
Sergeant Edgar F. Malone, Troop F, 10th Cavalry............2nd Lieutenant

130   HISTORY OF TENTH CAVALRY

Out of a total of fifty-seven non-commissioned officers sent to the training camp, forty-eight obtained commissions.

COMMISSIONED FROM TRAINING CAMP AT LEON SPRINGS, TEXAS.

Reg. Sgt. Major Eugene P. Frierson, 10th Cavalry..2nd Lieutenant
Sq. Sgt. Major John Coleman, 10th Cavalry..2nd Lieutenant

COMMISSIONED AS 2ND LIEUTENANTS OF CAVALRY, SEPTEMBER 27, 1918.

Sergeant William H. Marshall, Troop D, 10th Cavalry..2nd Lieutenant
Sergeant John C. Sanders, Troop D, 10th Cavalry..2nd Lieutenant
Sergeant Arthur Chambliss, Troop E, 10th Cavalry..2nd Lieutenant
Corporal James Everett, Troop E, 10th Cavalry...2nd Lieutenant
Corporal General Lee Grant, Troop H, 10th Cavalry..2nd Lieutenant
Sergeant Howard W. Fields, Troop L, 10th Cavalry..2nd Lieutenant
Sergeant Livingston J. Williams, Troop L, 10th Cavalry..2nd Lieutenant
Band Corporal John Clarke, Hq. Troop, 10th Cavalry...2nd Lieutenant
Sq. Sgt. Major Benjamin F. Preston, 10th Cavalry..2nd Lieutenant
Sergeant John A. Ford, Machine Gun Troop, 10th Cavalry....................................2nd Lieutenant
Sergeant Henry Clay Bennett, Supply Troop, 10th Cavalry....................................2nd Lieutenant
Band Leader William H. Lewis, 10th Cavalry...2nd Lieutenant

HEADQUARTERS TENTH CAVALRY,
Colonia Dublan, Mexico, July 1, 1916.

GENERAL ORDERS
No. 1

It becomes the sad duty of the Regimental Commander to announce the death in action with troops of the De Facto Government of Mexico at Carrizal, Chihuahua, Mexico, June 21, 1916, of

**CAPTAIN CHARLES T. BOYD and
FIRST LIEUTENANT HENRY R. ADAIR
Tenth Cavalry**

Capt. Boyd was born in Iowa October 29, 1970.

Was appointed to the Military Academy June 15, 1892, and graduated June 12, 1896. Was assigned to the 7th Cavalry same date as an additional 2d Lieutenant and on January 14, 1897, to the 4th Cavalry as a 2d Lieutenant. Was promoted to 1st Lieutenant on February 2d, 1901, and assigned to the 7th Cavalry. Transferred to the 4th Cavalry, May 2d, 1901. Promoted Capt. January 16, 1903, and assigned to the 10th Cavalry.

While a 2d Lieut. he was appointed Major 37th U. S. Infantry, and served as such from July 12, 1899, to Feb. 20, 1901.

He served with the 4th Cavalry and the 37th U. S. Infantry during the Philippine Insurrection.

Was Regimental Adjutant for four years.

Was a distinguished graduate of the School of the Line, 1912, and of the Army Staff College in 1916.

Lieut. Adair was born in Oregon April 13th, 1882.

Was appointed to the Military Academy August 1, 1900, graduated and assigned to the 10th Cavalry June 15, 1904.

Was promoted 1st Lieut. and reassigned to same regiment June 26, 1911.

Was a graduate of the Mounted Service School, first year's course, 1912, and second year's course, 1913.

During his service, all of which has been with the regiment, he has been Squadron Q. M. and Commissary, Squadron Adjutant and Acting Regtl. Adjutant at different time.

These officers met their death like the soldiers they were, leading their troopers under a heavy fire from a superior force. Capt. Boyd, although wounded twice, continued to lead the advance until he was felled by another bullet.

Lieut. Adair took command after Capt. Boyd's death and continued to direct the fire until he, too, was killed. They gallantly upheld the traditions of the 10th Cavalry.

The intrepid bravery and utter disregard of personal injury are characteristic of the military spirit and sense of duty of the two officers and afford an example worthy of emulation of every officer and man of the regiment.

The Regimental Commander voices the sentiment of the regiment in extending to the families and relatives of the deceased officers his heartfelt sympathy.

By order of Major Evans: S. McP. RUTHERFORD,
                               Capt. and Adjt., 10th Cavalry.
Official: S. McP. RUTHERFORD,
          Capt., and Adjt., 10th Cavalry.

APPENDIX "O"

Fort Sheridan, Illinois, December 28, 1920.

Dear Colonel Winans:

Your letter of the twenty-third received, in which you ask me to write something of my service at Huachuca.

When I reported for duty on July 4th, 1885, the post was garrisoned by four troops of the Fourth Cavalry and one company of the First Infantry Brevet Brigadier General George A. Forsythe, a former aide to General Sheridan, an officer of distinguished record during the Civil War and in the Indian campaigns, was in command. A month or so later Colonel William B. Royall, Colonel of the Fourth Cavalry, also a veteran of the Civil War and of the Mexican War, arrived and assumed command.

The four troops of cavalry were commanded by Wirt Davis, A. E. Wood, Henry W. Lawton and C. A. P. Hatfield. The infantry was commanded by Captain William N. Tisdall. They were a rugged, sturdy lot. All of them had had Civil War experience and long experience in the Indian campaigns in different parts of the western country.

General George Crook was in command of the department. We were in the midst of the Apache campaign, known as the Geronimo campaign, and were engaged in that phase of it which was commonly spoken of as the "Water-hole Campaign." The troops were stretched all along the frontier from the Whetstone Mountains east well into Mexico, guarding water-holes and passes. Communication was principally by telegraph or courier, with a certain number of heliograph stations.

The post was new and consisted of the old row of officers' quarters, which ran down to about the tip of the canyon on the east side. Opposite were the old cavalry barracks and stables. Enclosing the parade below was the post hospital, with its outbuildings. The trees were only a few feet high. The water all came from the springs up to the post canyon. We had plenty of it in rainy weather; often times it was short during the summer. There was a snug little hotel just across the creek up near where Sam the Chinaman (who was there at that time) now has his laundry.

The Tenth and the Fourth were in close cooperation during this campaign. The troops of the Tenth, under Lebo, Bill Davis, Carter Johnson, Ward, Grierson and others, were holding stations at Mescal Springs in the Whetstones; at Calabasas, under the Santa Ritas; at Crittenden; at Tempest Mine, just over the line in Sonora, and at La Noria. The Fourth had stations on the south side of the Huachucas, at Bisbee, at Skeleton Canyon and to the east, with a few troops at Camp Bowie.

The infantry was generally held in garrison, to take care of the post, although when the hard drive after Geronimo came in '86 about the hardest work of the whole campaign was done by organizations made up of selected officers and men from the Eighth Infantry.

Transportation was pack. The mounts in those days were better than any we have had since; and there was a knowledge of how to handle horses on the march which is lacking in our cavalry service, as a whole, today. Most of the officers then had seen service in the Civil War. They knew how to get mounted commands over great stretches of country, and to bring in their animals in good condition.

The country was full of alarms and troops were scurrying hither and thither in an attempt to pick up the trail of small raiding groups of Apaches. It was a hard-working, wholesome and interesting life. There was an excellent regimental esprit and pride in the service. It was the beginning of the end of our hard Indian work in the southwest. In those strenuous days the Tenth Cavalry played a fine part, a part highly creditable to officers and men.

The Tenth was in my brigade (the first dismounted cavalry brigade) at Santiago; it was made up of the First and Tenth Regulars and the First Volunteer Cavalry, commonly known as the Rough Riders. This brigade constituted the American force at the fight at Las Guasimas. Additional cavalry and infantry came up just after we had dislodged the Spanish. At the big fight, which was a big one, as it was the determining battle of the campaign, on July 1st at San Juan Ridge, just outside the city of Santiago, the brigade made an excellent record, it and the Second Cavalry Brigade carrying and holding a long section of the enemy's lines. In both actions the work of the Tenth Cavalry was excellent.

The relations between the Tenth Cavalry and the Fourth were excellent and were characterized by a friendly rivalry. The permanent station of most of the Tenth at that time was Camp Grant, with a troop or two at Camp Thomas. Transportation was via the old Guaymas railroad, and everything came up from what was known as The Siding. The present railroad was not built into the post until about 1911 or '12, and the Post Gardens were principally in Garden Canyon, from which most of the water now comes. The reservation had approximately its present limits.

The service at Huachuca and in the field in the old days was a good school for officers and men. It was a healthy, vigorous life. I feel sure the Tenth Cavalry has in it today men who were in it in the eighties, and that you will find Huachuca a pleasant post to serve at, with excellent opportunities for training.

The Tenth is a fine regiment and I congratulate you on being in command of it.

Very sincerely yours,
(Signed) LEONARD WOOD.

"THROUGH THE CHAPARRAL AND SAND"

APPENDIX "P"

General Pershing contributed this valuable letter for a special number of the regimental weekly, the "Buffalo Bulletin:"

GENERAL OF THE ARMIES, WASHINGTON

January 8, 1921.

Colonel Edwin B. Winans,
    Commanding Tenth U. S. Cavalry,
        Fort Huachuca, Arizona.

My Dear Colonel Winans:

I am glad and honored to contribute something for a special number of the Tenth Cavalry Bulletin. Many years have passed—twenty-two, to be exact—since my last service in the Tenth, but my mind is filled with recollections of those days in the Old Army, days of as much excitement as in the new, and possibly more variety.

The regiment was at Fort Assiniboine in October, 1895, when I first joined and reported for duty with D Troop. The Pine Ridge campaign a few years before had closed the era of Indian warfare on the plains, and the scattered units of the little Regular Army awaited in their frontier posts of their late campaign, the next phase of our national development, which was to carry them overseas to battle with a European power.

Meanwhile, in the summer of 1896, several troops of the regiment were sent to round up a number of bands of Cree Indians who had crossed the international boundary following the suppression of their rebellion in Canada. Troop D, under my command, took a leading part in this task, doing some hard riding to overtake or surprise bands located in Montana and Idaho, sending some by rail to Canada, and finally escorting a band of some six hundred across the border.

My troop required little of its officers. The ranks were filled with veterans and the power and prestige of the old top sergeant was sufficient to maintain rigid discipline and manage the minor details of administration. Almost perfect at drill, most of our interest centered in keen competition on the rifle range and in hunting.

I recall a visit of General Nelson A. Miles, then Commander of the Army, which was largely spent in hunting the game which abounded in the vicinity of the post. As a result of this visit I was soon afterwards relieved from duty with the regiment and assigned to his office in Washington.

The concentration of troops for the Spanish-American War in 1898 carried the Tenth to Chickamauga, where I joined as Regimental Quartermaster, and thence to Tampa. Landing at Siboney on June 23rd, we were almost immediately involved in the preliminary skirmish of the war, in company with the Rough Riders. The following days were strenuous and exciting, culminating in the charge up San Juan Hill. Here I rejoined my old troop, D, which had covered itself with glory in the heaviest of the fighting.

The Battle of Santiago was a small affair, a mere skirmish in comparison with out recent experiences, but it tried the valor and endurance of the strongest men, and our casualties were very heavy. The splendid discipline of the Regular Army made possible the success gained despite inconceivable confusion, lack of preparation and material, and the old veterans of the Tenth became famous throughout the country for their fine performance on that battlefield.

This terminated my association with the regiment, but I have never forgotten the valuable lessons learned at the time, and I shall always look back with affection and pleasure to my days in the Tenth Cavalry.

To you and your officers and men I send my warmest regards and best wishes for the New Year.

Very sincerely yours,
JOHN J. PERSHING.

THE TENTH CAVALRY IN MEXICO

From U. S. Cavalry Journal of October, 1917.

By Captain O. C. Troxel, Tenth Cavalry.

There have appeared in the Service Journals at various times, articles dealing with special phases of our experiences in Mexico, covering some action in which a particular troop or troops were engaged, equipment of troops, sanitation, or what not, but I have seen none that dealt in any way with the work of cavalry along its broader lines—that of pushing well out to the front, separating itself from its friendly troops, continuing its work while relying absolutely on the country for its sustenance, and operating in name and in fact as Independent Cavalry. Whatever phases of cavalry work our cavalry in Mexico did not get, certainly none will deny that we did get the part mentioned above. In this article, however, I purpose limiting myself to the one phase of how we "lived on the country," and certainly no cavalryman who served in Mexico is more justified in saying that he did ALL the things mentioned above than the members of the Tenth Cavalry who composed the expedition to near Parral under Colonel W. C. Brown, then in command of the regiment.

I speak of the Second Squadron and Machine Gun Troop, Tenth Cavalry, which served in Mexico from March 20th to April 22nd without one mouthful of Government rations, one grain or spear of Government forage, one cent of Government money, no Government clothing, nor aid of any kind; and when on May 1st, 1916, it arrived back at San Antonio, Mexico, from the south, it was truly a case of survival of the fittest, for there had been no picking of officers, men or horses for any part of the expedition.

We had, from 6 p. m. March 9th to about 7:45 p. m. April 12th, passed over 750 miles of road space from Fort Huachuca, Arizona, to Santa Cruz de Villegas, near Parral, in twenty-eight marching days. This of course does not measure the extra work done by those men and horses on advance, rear and flank guards, patrols, foraging parties, etc. They were what remained of the same troops that had left Fort Huachuca on March 9th with wagon and pack trains. There had, however, been certain changes in personnel over which we had no control. Our wagons were left at Culberson's ranch, the sick men and horses were left at Colonia Dublan, our pack train was, on April 5th, ordered back to Namiquipa to procure supplies for us, and we continued south, retaining one mule per troop. Our sick men and sick animals at that time were sent north with the pack train. There were no further changes in personnel, except for the occasional buying of a horse or mule to keep the command mounted.

Our march overland to Culberson's ranch was in no sense severe, but the weather was hot; only now and then did we have hay, watering facilities were always poor, the supply insufficient, and frequently none except at our nightly camps, and the country was sandy and devoid of grazing. We thus marched 160 miles before we entered Mexico. We lost several horses from sand colic and all horses had begun to feel the effects of the march.

At this place we were joined by the Seventh Cavalry, and Battery B, Fifth Field Artillery, and with packed saddles for officers and men, five days' rations and three pack trains, made the march to Colonia Dublan, a distance of something over 100 miles, from shortly after midnight of March 15-16 to the evening of the 17th. On the evening of the 18th the Tenth Cavalry received orders to turn over to the Seventh Cavalry all of its remaining rations, and the Seventh left camp at 3 a. m. At about 6 a. m. March 19th we received orders to receive rations in the hands of Battery B and entrain for the south. This battery had already eaten half of their five days' rations for three and two-thirds days. As there were not enough freight cars for Troops I and K, only Regimental Headquarters, First and Second Squadrons, Machine Gun Troop and the Pack Train were entrained. Troops L and M had not joined.

Our troubles in patching and nailing up the cars, getting material for camps, collecting wood for the wood-burning engine and getting started late in the afternoon with the animals inside the freight cars and the officers and men on top in truly Mexican style, were exceeded, if possible, only by the troubles in keeping the engine going by having the men get off and chop mesquite to burn in it, only to find that the wood must be used to send the engine some place for water, and so on ad infinitum.

As a result, all but the First Squadron detained at about 11 a m March 20th at El Rucio, about twenty-seven miles out of Dublan For this noon meal we ate the last of our Government rations, except perhaps some flour, and our pack train carried only oats From this day on we were to be "on the country" Each officer had a small amount of money Personally I had something less than $10, but I had fortified myself with a check book which was to prove of no use to me as we were to strike only one place (Cusi) where money could be obtained for checks At first we had not much trouble in getting supplies in exchange for receipts given by the quartermaster, but as we went further south the natives became poorer and more reluctant to part with their supplies for a possible 'scrap of paper," and one cannot blame them

Considering all the varied circumstances of our being in Mexico, what should we do? To further embitter the Mexican people by taking away almost their last food and forage and not replace it with currency which they knew to be good and with which they could replace the stores taken, seemed to be the action to be taken only as a last resort It was then that Colonel Brown began giving his personal checks for supplies taken, and continued doing so until his totals aggregated something like $1,680 00 We were so entirely dependent on the country, especially as we had to depend each night on the supplies where we happened to be, since we had no pack train, that I do not believe we could have continued south as we did had it not been for this assistance

As to rations and cooking after leaving Colonia Dublan. We entered Mexico with no other cooking utensils than three camp kettles per squadron, and, with five troops (we separated from the First Squadron on the morning of April 1st) this gave each troop a kettle three days out of five This was run by roster among the mess sergeants Later, as we were able to find them, kerosene oil cans were purchased at $1 00 apiece, which helped materially.

The only articles of food that we could get regularly were beef and frijoles—very seldom could we get even a poor quality of flour or corn meal. However, when we could get corn in sufficient quantities to justify us in taking it from the horses, I made a practice of sending out scouts to locate little hand-mills about the size of coffee-mills, and had corn ground up for meal The details often worked way into the night, but the great tendency was to grind too coarsely and thus get quantity instead of quality, with resultant cramps and diarrhoeal effects among the men This, ground, was mixed with water and fried into cakes, which the men generally made too thick, and, therefore, not being well cooked, were very indigestible We were seldom able to get lard or salt, and when we got the latter it was common dirty stock salt (rock) and little chunks of it would appear in the eating. Baking powder was impossible either on account of its absence or cost Sugar and coffee were practically out of the question Individuals could at times obtain a small quantity of burnt Mexican coffee, and were glad to have it even without the sugar There were a few eggs, but they were expensive, and the difficult part was in making change for small purchases as there seemed to be no change in the country We were always crazy for fruits, jams and sweets of any kind, and practically nothing of this kind was to be had When on the few occasions sugar was obtainable, one could always see men eating it just so I never allowed meat bones to be thrown away After cutting off the meat as best we could with pocket knives or mess knives for individual cooking, the bones would be carried to the next camp, and if we were to have the kettle that night they would be put on to boil, and boiled all night over the fire kept up by the picket line guard About an hour before reveille the cooks would be awakened and they would add from three to five cups (three was sufficient) of ground corn, and then just before serving, scrape off all meat from the bones, stir up well and serve This breakfast was fit for a king, to our minds, and was much enjoyed by all I have eaten nothing equal to it either before or since and I hope I never have to, but it was good then

We generally had our beans (frijoles) for breakfast as there was not time in camp to prepare them for any other meal Even then the altitude was so high that they could not be thoroughly cooked, and so there were more digestive troubles We tried grinding up wheat for use in making bread, but it did not seem to serve as well Personally I am very fond of parched corn and nearly always started out in the morning with a pocket full and would have nothing else to eat till night "Parched corn coffee" also was much better than water.

As to clothing: Each man started with the authorized allowance in his pack. Unfortunately the men had gotten so used to going out for border duty and wearing their oldest clothes that many did the same thing this time. This made conditions worse than they should have been. Hoods of stirrups were used to tack on as half-soles of shoes, when tacks were available. Breeches were patched so long as patches would hold together, the men gambling to see whose shelter half was to be cut up for the purpose. Occasionally the quartermaster bought and issued civilian clothing of all descriptions, and for hats the men took the lining of the saddle bags, in the cases where hats were lost or completely torn up. I got my patches from the lining of my overcoat.

As to horses: Fodder was often unobtainable and when at hand was generally insufficient in quantity. There was practically no grazing except the dry grass as it lay dead on the ground. The horses would eat this for about half an hour and then stand with hanging heads or lie down. No oats was in the country, and corn was generally insufficient. Instead of getting about twelve cups per day they had often for days at a time only three or four per horse. Occasionally we had to feed wheat, which seemed to cause flatulency, but I do not remember any bad case of colic in my troop due to it. At one camp we had only corn ground on the cob, and mostly cob, to feed. We lost a number of horses the following day from inability to keep up. At all halts I had my horse unbridled and led to the best place in the vicinity for grazing. Every opportunity was taken to water them, and often the distances between watering places were so great that one was hard put to it to decide whether to let them drink the strong alkali water met with or wait hoping for something better. I, personally, saw to it that at least twice a week the horses were held for a time in the water for the purpose of soaking and cooling their feet. I also found it necessary to pick out the places for and supervise the grazing, and I do not care to answer the criticisms of officers whom I have heard condemn this as being the work of a non-commissioned officer. It is shorter and more to the point to say that such officers are simply too lazy to do it.

As for horseshoes, the horseshoer had his emergency equipment and each man had one fore and one hind shoe (fitted). I learned afterwards what I probably would not have approved at the time, and that is that my horseshoer (a new man, too) had taken sixteen extra shoes in his saddle bags. These latter came in handy. At each halt the horseshoer and his assistant, one assigned to each platoon, stood ready to tighten shoes as called for by the riders, whose first duty at each halt was to examine their horses shoes with that object in view.

I made each man feel that I would do my utmost to prevent his walking so long as his horse was not laid up through being barefooted or having a sore back, and impressed it on them that I would do nothing for them in such cases, if investigation showed them to have been neglectful, and that in any case the individual whose horse became unserviceable from any cause was out of luck. The result was that grooming and saddling became of very great importance to them and each squad leader inspected the horses of his squad and reported to me that they were or were not in such and such condition and pointed the individual horses out to me that needed attention. This was in addition to the inspection that both the farrier and myself made. Also no cast-off horseshoe was ever passed by when marching at a walk. That was one thing for which I always granted permission to fall out, and the only other time when I gave this permission was after I had personally had a detailed explanation of the necessity therefor. The men soon stopped asking. There was, however, one article that we could not make up and that was the horseshoe nail, but, thanks to the high, dry altitude, we were troubled little, if any, by rust, as each man carried them in a greasy rag.

On April 10th we were ordered to turn all our horseshoes into a common pile for the common good of the command. This was heartrending to the men as well as to myself to give up our hoarding, but I was proud to see something like thirty-five shoes turned in by my troop of forty-three men. One other troop turned in a similar quantity, and one troop turned in one shoe. It is easy to determine which troop was the cause of the order and which one got the most shoes from the pile, but still it was a necessary thing to do. We had no forge and tools for fitting and shoeing, but could occasionally get some assistance from the very incomplete blacksmith shops at ranches. The first real opportunity for fitting shoes and trimming the feet was down near Parral when we were able to borrow an outfit from the troops of the Eleventh Cavalry that joined us there under Colonel Allen and Major Howze. Undoubtedly a great deal of the fatigue experienced by our horses was due to their long hoof walls, none of which had been trimmed nor to which had shoes been properly fitted at least since March 15th—one month before. We had the old model equipment and depended on lariats entirely for the picket line. Broken lariats were never thrown away but tied together many times for re-use or used for halter tie ropes.

On our way back from Parral corn was generally plentiful and we had some hay. I heard much comment as to the advisability of putting the animals on full feed at once. For me that was decided by my stable sergeant. The horses had had a full feed at night and were to have a full feed in the morning, but in addition to these feeds of corn there was some wheat for which we would have no transportation the following day. He, in disobedience to my orders, got up at 2 a. m. and fed the wheat rather than leave it. I wanted to try him by court-martial but awaited results. The result was that I became a convert to the Indian's method of "eating all you can while you have it, and starve when you have to," when it comes to feeding hard working horses. I also adopted the same motto for the pale face.

During the return march north from San Antonio a very curious thing developed. Prior to May 1st I had not had a sore back in my troop—not a man had walked on this account. At San Antonio we rested for three or four days, and again at Lake Itascate. It was at this latter place that I noticed some of the withers thickening and becoming quite hard, eventually requiring the lance, and while the horses were doing absolutely nothing. It was a great surprise to me at the time, and if crying could have done any good I think I would have tried it. To think that this should have happened after the trouble and pains taken! On sober thought I realized that it was just what I might have expected. However, there were only a few of these and none broke out after we started to use the horses again.

After separating from the First Squadron on April 1st, with whom we did not again join until about May 14th at Namiquipa, we had a very pretty action against Villistas. We struck them at about 1:30 p. m. They had undoubtedly already begun to retreat and our action was with their rear guard only. They opened up at longe range on Troop E, (Capt. S. D. Smith), our advance guard. We could see them leaving the village of Aguas Calicutes and turn to the left around a low mountain peak. Troop F (Capt. W. S. Valentine) was sent across the saddle, hoping to head them off on our extreme left; I, with Troop H, was sent up over this peak just to the left of the village, Major Chas. Young accompanying me; the Machine Gun Troop (Captain A. E. Phillips) went forward to take care of the ridge to the immediate right of the village, and Troop G (Captain Geo. B. Rodney) was rear guard and escort for the pack train, was for the moment held until it was learned that they were melting away in our front. Having gained the peak and finding no enemy, I got word from Captain Valentine that he was engaged further to my left, and pulled my troop off in that direction. My troop remained in line of foragers at the trot and came up on Captain Valentine's left rear and continued in the oblique direction so that eventually Captain Valentine's front was covered, leaving him free to mount and follow, which he promptly did. Troops E, G and machine guns went on through the town.

When the Mexicans saw my reinforcing troop they scattered and their fire became much more diminished. It was all going wild, so that my troop continued at the trot in hopes of striking the main body. I finally saw what appeared to be about one hundred and fifty men about two miles ahead. I assembled my troops on ground favorable for rapid movements, sent a message to Colonel Brown and went after them at the gallop, closely followed by Captain Valentine. The "cracks" of their rifles began sounding pretty frequently again, and we formed foragers and later dismounted for fire action, but soon saw that that was not the proper thing to do. By this time F Troop was alongside and we pursued them up to a horseshoe shaped ridge at the top of which they were seemingly to make a stand. Captain Valentine went off to the right and I dismounted one platoon under first sergeant, and with the other advanced at the gallop under his fire to the end of the horseshoe, by which time the Mexican's fire had ceased and, as we later found out, they disappeared from the face of the earth to meet us on many occasions afterwards as perfectly good, loyal Carrancistas. Having gained the ridge all trace of them was gone. We began riding in ever increasing circles until we found where they assembled in sufficient numbers to make a trail. We followed this over the ridge and down to a ranch (Mestena) on the other side, where the people claimed that about one hundred and fifty Villistas had passed It was then probably about 5 p m Messengers were sent to Colonel Brown and Captain Valentine, and we prepared to stay there for the night The other troops came in about 8 p m We never saw these Villistas as opponents again I made no notes at the time and have been unable to get data from others at this late date, so I will not try to give any figures However, none of our men were hit and the horses were the only part of our command that had not enjoyed the skirmish One horse was wounded, one of mine dropped exhausted, one died that night, we killed one the next morning, and one could just get along by being led I do not know the loss of the animals in other troops.

We captured several ponies and mules and a part of their pack train. We know of three Mexicans killed, and reports from Mexican sources, as noted in American papers, gave their casualties as forty-two, but I doubt the number and do not believe any of our officers think we got that many. As they were never out in the open, and as it was a running fight, we had no opportunity to look for their casualties nor did we particularly care to do so

I have wished many times that I had deliberately kept such notes as would have enabled me to give real data—figures and dates—covering our experiences, especially as to horses, their forage, shoeing, condition, etc, so that this might have been an article from which more valuable information could be gleaned for our future operations such as will undoubtedly come to our cavalry

However, should I be ordered out on exactly the same proposition again, and know that I had the same problems to face in the same high, dry altitude, and with the same strict allowance, I would beg my commanding officer for one more mule per troop (making a total of two) and about two mules per squadron to carry such as one forge and one set of blacksmith tools and a small quantity of farriers, saddlers and medical supplies I would also want some money, unless I was operating in a hostile country and could take full advantage of that fact This, of course, presupposes that the squadron will stay together, and as a matter of fact it need never be so far separated that each troop can not occasionally take advantage of the articles on the two squadron mules

After returning to Dublan the officers of the regiment were called together and required to vote on what cavalry actually needed for just such operations and the transportation necessary for this purpose Again I do not remember figures, but I do remember that we could have, by our votes, been divided into three distinct classes, depending on the experiences passed through, viz: First, those who did not engage in any scouting operations, second, those who mostly made trips from some base, out and back on some special mission, third, those composing the expedition south under Colonel Brown The first class voted for much more plunder and transportation than the other two, and the third class the least of all

APPENDIX "Q"

HEADQUARTERS TENTH CAVALRY

Fort Huachuca, Arizona, June 24, 1921

Memorandum

1 The following letter is published for the information of the command

HEADQUARTERS EIGHTH CORPS AREA

Fort Sam Houston, Texas, June 20, 1921

From The Adjutant
To Colonel Edwin B Winans, Tenth Cavalry, Fort Huachuca, Arizona.
Subject Commendation

The following extract from report of inspection of Fort Huachuca, Arizona made by Lieut Colonel W V Morris, Inspector General, April 26-May 2 1921, is furnished you under A. R 20-25 (11).

Colonel E. B Winans, Tenth Cavalry, is worthy of commendation for the improvement in the condition of the Tenth Cavalry since the last annual inspection The appearance, uniformity and completeness of equipment were excellent To Colonel Winans is also due much of the credit for the excellent morale, and esprit of the regiment On the whole, I consider the Tenth Cavalry to be as good, and in some respects better, than the Thirteenth Cavalry, which up to this time, was in the best condition of any regiment I had ever inspected.

By command of Major General Dickman:

A. E. SAXTON,
Adjutant.

2. In publishing this commendation to the regiment, the commanding officer desires to say that officers and men are entitled to equal share in the credit, for without their cooperation, such a showing would have been impossible.

EDWIN B. WINANS,
Colonel, Tenth Cavalry, Commanding.

APPENDIX "R"

The following contribution is from the pen of Colonel Frank R. McCoy, ex-Second and First Lieutenant, of this regiment. His record in the A. E. F. as Lieutenant Colonel, Colonel and Brigadier is well known.

SPECIAL MISSION TO THE PHILIPPINE ISLANDS
Malacanan Palace, Manila, P. I., June 11th, 1921.

Major. E. L. N. Glass, Tenth Cavalry, Fort Huachuca, Arizona.

Dear Major: For some time I have been enjoying the Buffalo Bulletin with many a smile of a good green remembrance, and for all of that time I have been intending to write you and express my thanks and continued interest. Just before leaving the States, I received your letter asking for some reminiscences, so that now being in a peaceful mood for a change, I shall be glad to call up some old friends and incidents of my service in Cuba with the Tenth Cavalry.

The regiment was in camp at Chickamauga Park in April of '98, when Lieutenant T. A. Roberts and I, both of the class of '97, and having served in the Seventh and Eighth Cavalry, respectively, joined from those regiments left behind, from which we were lucky enough to obtain transfers to the Tenth, then on the way to the fight in Cuba. I joined A Troop, under Lieutenant R. L. Livermore of fragrant memory, and on one of the last days Colonel Guy V. Henry was in command. I remember the day of my arrival. We were ordered to mount up and call upon the colonels and officers of the other cavalry regiments in camp, and I got my first impression of the dash and spirit of the regiment as we went over at full gallop to call on the Second, a fine, bold lot and full of fighting spirit from the Colonel down, and what is more, they looked the part. There wasn't a fat dub in the outfit. Even among this lean lot, Colonel Guy V. Henry, Colonel Wint, Jones, Ayres, Watson, Pershing, Paxton, Shipp, Smith, Whitehead, Kennington, Vidmer, Livermore, the two new lieutenants were referred to and bets laid that they were thinner than Vidmer who up to that time held undisputed honors for the best and thinnest cavalry legs, although Captain Charles G. Ayres had his opinion as to which were the most shapely and the best booted and spurred.

My first night around the camp fire was a most agreeable one and I shall always look back on the associations started there, the high spirit and the wide range of fun and interest. Ayres twirled his mustaches and held that his father, General Ayres, was a grand soldier and looked the part—"even in his shirt tail he looked like the God of War," and he modestly informed us youngsters that he was very like his father. Not only Charles G., but all others in the regiment soon proved their worth and wear in the hard campaign in Cuba, and have left an abiding pride and pleasure of association.

Lieutenant Pershing left us after the Santiago campaign and was succeeded as quartermaster by Lieutenant Harbord. Many of the other generals of the late war, such as Barnum, Hay, Rockenbach, and a number of the most gallant and able colonels, such as Bruce Palmer, Whitehead, Vidmer, Whitesides, Short and Gordon Johnson, served with the regiment during the military occupation of Cuba, and got their experience in colonial and other work there. In recalling all these beloved comrades, I think of my own captain, Beck, whom I first saw chasing our transport in Tampa Bay reporting from sick leave in spite of orders to stay sick, and climbing a rope tossed overboard the good ship Leona, bound for Santiago. He had been a captain of cavalry thirty-five years before and had commanded Sherman's bodyguard in the March to the Sea, and he served through the Santiago campaign as a captain, but one full of experience and real leadership on the battlefield, that I for one shall always be grateful for having benefitted by during that campaign. The last time I saw the old Colonel was when in the War College he sent for me to come to the hospital at Washington Barracks, and I found him propped up in bed smoking a pipe, cheerful and cool as ever, and asked me to stand by him while he had his leg cut off. Nothing ever feazed that sturdy old soldier, whether on the battlefield or under the hack of the surgeon. His only remark to me when I was knocked out on San Juan Hill, was a casual glance at my wounded leg and a smile, "Well, McCoy, you are safe. The Spaniards are not good enough marksmen to hit you again,' and then just as casually asked me for my field glasses and pouchful of tobacco as he trudged off to the front line where he organized the scattered remnants of various regiments and made dispositions for holding the hill against counter-attacks. Major Stephen Norvell, the Squadron Command, was another gallant veteran of the Civil War whom I shall always look back on with pride and pleasure. Lieutenant Roberts, my side partner and dearest friend, was also knocked out at Santiago by a Mauser bullet through the stomach, and after applying first aid to himself, wrote me a little line, a will and farewell, leaving his shicker to Smith and his tobacco to me but, thank Heaven, he pulled through to fight many a good fight since and to command another black regiment with distinguished success in France. Pendergast was first sergeant of A Troop, then one of the best shots in the Army, and did some effective shooting of Spaniards when they were trying to reform and reattack San Juan Hill on the afternoon of July 1st. Carter Smith, Smith Johnson, Taylor, Saddler Adams, Blue who was wounded at the same time I was and is still a sergeant in the Army with an excellent record in France, Corporal Wiley Hipshur, who was left in charge of my Gordon setter and the packs of the trroop thrown off under the balloon near the Bloody Bend, and who walked up and down in the very hottest part of the battlefield all that day until wounded, and Parker, who looked after all the wounded with faithful and effective care, all come to my mind with warm feelings of remembrance. Charles A Lewis, who was one of the young rookies of that campaign, I saw the other day as a sergeant of the Ninth Cavalry while we were playing polo at Camp Stotsenburg. The most picturesque character in the regiment in those days was Carter Johnson, who remained in it until he was retired at Fort Robinson. The regiment will always cherish his memory and fighting qualities with many a laugh at his eccentricities, adventures and misadventures. Some day the regimental history must have the account of his foray in Cuba in the summer of 98 with the picked troop that took in arms and supplies to Gomez, not forgetting the fight at Arroyo Blanco where he had a fight with General Gomez as well as with the Spaniards, and pulled down the Cuban flag from the flagpole, and having no American flag at hand, ran up his blue blouse as a sign of capture, and threatened to shoot the first man that attempted to lower it. But he would require a whole book to himself.

I must end these rambling reminiscences with a heart full of thanks to you and your colonel for the reviving of the old time spirit of the regiment and showing it in so many soldierly ways. If it was the proper time and place, I could spin many a yarn about the present colonel of the regiment, for I served alongside of him through those great months of September October and November of 1918, and when we are old enough soldiers to turn loose and tell the story of the Great War, General Winans and his Wisconsin brigade will touch the high spots when it comes to writing of the hot fighting of Juvigny and the break through the Kriemhilde Stellung on Le Cote Dame Marie in the Argonne.

With my best hows and best wishes for you both and good luck to the regiment.

Very sincerely yours,

FRANK M'COY

OFFICERS OF THE REGIMENT, NOVEMBER, 1920

THE "OLD TIMERS"; THE BACKBONE OF THE REGIMENT

FIELD AND STAFF OFFICERS, NOVEMBER, 1920

CORNER OF OFFICERS' CLUB, FT. HUACHUCA

PRINTED BY
ACME PRINTING COMPANY
TUCSON, ARIZONA
1921

Univ Calif - Dig

e obtained